Fabian Society
11 Dartmouth Street
London SW1H 9BN
www.fabians.org.uk

Editorial Director: Tom Hampson
Editorial Manager: Ed Wallis

Foundation for European Progressive Studies
Rue Montoyer 40
1000 Brussels, Belgium
www.feps-europe.eu

Policy Advisor: Ania Skrzypek

A FEPS/Fabian Book
First published 2011
ISBN 978 0 7163 4112 3

British Library Cataloguing in Publication data.
A catalogue record for this book is available from the
British Library.

Printed and bound by DG3

Europe's Left in the Crisis

How the next left can respond

Jessica Asato, David Coats, Caroline Gennez,
Alfred Gusenbauer, and Roger Liddle

Edited by Sunder Katwala and Ernst Stetter

With new YouGov polling

FOUNDATION FOR EUROPEAN
PROGRESSIVE STUDIES
FONDATION EUROPÉENNE
D'ÉTUDES PROGRESSISTES

The Fabian Society

The Fabian Society is Britain's leading left of centre think tank and political society, committed to creating the political ideas and policy debates which can shape the future of progressive politics.

With over 300 Fabian MPs, MEPs, Peers, MSPs and AMs, the Society plays an unparalleled role in linking the ability to influence policy debates at the highest level with vigorous grassroots debate among our growing membership of over 7000 people, 70 local branches meeting regularly throughout Britain and a vibrant Young Fabian section and Fabian Women's Network. Fabian publications, events and ideas therefore reach and influence a wider audience than those of any comparable think tank. The Society is unique among think tanks in being a thriving, democratically-constituted membership organisation, affiliated to the Labour Party but organisationally and editorially independent.

For over 120 years Fabians have been central to every important renewal and revision of left of centre thinking. The Fabian commitment to open and participatory debate is as important today as ever before as we explore the ideas, politics and policies which will define the next generation of progressive politics in Britain, Europe and around the world. To find out more about the Fabian Society, the Young Fabians, the Fabian Women's Network and our local societies, please visit our web site at **www.fabians.org.uk**.

Joining the Fabians is easy
For more information about joining the Fabian Society and to learn more about our recent publications, please turn to the final page.

Foundation for European Progressive Studies

FEPS is the first progressive political foundation established at the European level. Created in 2007 and co-financed by the European Parliament, it aims at establishing an intellectual crossroad between social democracy and the European project. It puts fresh thinking at the core of its action and serves as an instrument for pan-European intellectual and political reflection.

Acting as a platform for ideas, FEPS relies first and foremost on a network of members composed of more than 40 national political foundations and think tanks from all over the EU. The Foundation also closely collaborates with a number of international correspondents and partners in the world that share the ambition to foster research, promote debate and spread the progressive thinking.

www.feps-europe.eu

You can also find FEPS on

 Facebook

 Twitter

 Netvibes

FOUNDATION FOR EUROPEAN
PROGRESSIVE STUDIES
FONDATION EUROPÉENNE
D'ÉTUDES PROGRESSISTES

Contents

Contributors

Editors

Sunder Katwala is General Secretary of the Fabian Society.

Ernst Stetter is Secretary General of FEPS.

Authors

Roger Liddle is chair of Policy Network and a Labour member of the House of Lords.

Alfred Gusenbauer is Chair of the FEPS 'Next Left' Research Programme and former Chancellor of Austria.

Caroline Gennez is party leader of Sp.a, the Flemish social democrats in Belgium.

David Coats is the founder and director of WorkMatters Consulting and a research fellow at the Smith Institute.

Jessica Asato is director of the Labour YES! campaign for electoral reform and was social media organiser for the David Miliband Labour leadership campaign.

Foreword

Ernst Stetter

"Peace, like freedom, is not an original state which existed from the start; we shall have to make it, in the truest sense of the word," said Willy Brandt, the German Chancellor, who 40 years ago dropped to his knees in front of the monument commemorating the Warsaw Ghetto Uprising. This symbolic gesture began a new era which – with its acknowledgement of the post-war borders and new politics of Eastern Europe – laid the foundations for the united Europe of today.

It is important to evoke this outstanding and courageous example today, when a ruling conservative majority claims Europe's entire past and present while also seeking to monopolise the debate about its future.

In an age of great anxiety, intensified by all the human misery brought about by the last economic crisis, progressives have a historic duty to re-establish themselves as the democratically legitimised representatives of the people. As Willy Brandt proved, it has always been – and shall remain – the mission of progressives to stand for equality, fairness, freedom and solidarity. And in times when these values are overshadowed by fear and greedy individualism, it is crucial to restore hope in them and to place them at the core of a new social contract. This book is a collection of groundbreaking, constructive thoughts on how to achieve it.

This publication reflects a common effort by FEPS – the Foundation for European Progressive Studies – and the

Fabian Society. Both progressive think tanks have been working together on the 'Next Left' research programme which was launched after the disastrous results of the European Elections in 2009. Next Left tries to provide answers to three primary questions.

The first is an assessment of the crisis of the European project itself. The last European elections saw the lowest turnout since direct European parliamentary elections began and the outcome was, even by the standards of the European Parliament, the most fragmented chamber yet. Europe, which had not yet recovered from its recent institutional crisis, was further hit by the economic crisis. This exposed the monetary vulnerability of its member states. Paradoxically, instead of applying a common strategy based on solidarity, the EU moved towards the implementation of 27 diverse plans in the spirit of out-dated conceptions of a Europe of nations. Indeed it is already common knowledge that globalisation made it impossible for one state alone to determine all its policies. At a micro-level, the austerity measures which were applied served to antagonise societies – workers stood against workers, employed against unemployed, younger against older. All these observations have been reflected in the work of the FEPS 'Next Left' project. The researchers and politicians involved have aimed to answer the questions posed by a changing society and to detect what a new progressive socio-economic paradigm for Europe should be – and this is very much evident in Roger Liddle's and David Coats's chapters in this book.

The second question relates to the place of Europe in the world. The values that inspired the European integration process at its birth were peace and solidarity. Subsequent generations of social democrats enriched them through the introduction of concepts such as sustainable development and multilateral global governance. But the recent crisis has exposed the fact that these are not the prevailing values; instead, there is a worldwide diktat by capital and markets which are not subordinate to rules or democratic control. This is the defining factor in strengthening multinational corporations and weakening the people, whose voices remain unheard as the decision-making process is systematically transferred from world intergovernmental organisations to other self-appointed forums: the G2, G8 or G20.

Europe's place in the world, additionally, is no longer what it was in the last century. Together with the decline of its GDP contribution, its policy-making strength is also shrinking substantially relative to the 'emerging powers'. What's more, despite the Lisbon Treaty that put in place the High Representative for Foreign Affairs and Security, Europe is still unable to unite in the name of a common external policy agenda. It is clear that the post-war order, as it had been known, is over. In this context, there is a need for a new vision and new policies, for which it is imperative to generate broad public support. The Next Left research programme – as well as this book – aims to offer related and intriguing viewpoints.

Finally, naturally the main focus of the intellectual process that FEPS and the Fabian Society have led is social democracy itself. In its 160 year history it has observed many turbulent moments, which often resulted in splits in the movement. In certain decades it led to the establishment of new organisations; in others it brought intense ideological debate about the way forward. The most recent pan-European debate on the movement's future took place within the scope of the 'third way', which readapted social democracy to the challenges of the 21st century. Over a decade later – now this 'golden age' of social democracy is over – it seems that the task to renew social democracy is a mission to preserve a democratic order in Europe. It can no longer be taken for granted that well established parties with long traditions will remain on the political stage. The available space is aggressively claimed by the extremists and populists, who mobilise their support by preying on people's fears and taking advantage of people's increasing detachment from politics. For social democrats, the challenge is to come up with a modern and adequate interpretation of traditional values; to reorganise, to re-establish a wide progressive alliance and to regain credibility. This is therefore a question of whether 'to be or not to be'. Finding the appropriate answers has been an inspiration both for the Next Left research programme, as well as for Jessica Asato and Alfred Gusenbauer in this book.

The overarching theme of this collection is the need for social democrats, and subsequently society, to change and to establish a new kind of social contract. Here, FEPS and the Fabian Society attempt to provide a common framework for this.

Ernst Stetter
FEPS Secretary General

1. Introduction
Sunder Katwala

In this age of European austerity, Europe's left finds itself on the sidelines, not in the driving seat. The political right commands the political and economic agenda. A global recession, caused by the bursting of a financial bubble, has been reframed as a crisis of excessive public spending. A failure to regulate has ended up being about the over-reach of government. If the multilateral response to the immediate crisis in the autumn of 2008 and spring of 2009 succeeded in preventing systemic collapse and a 1929-style global slump, hopes of a co-ordinated plan for economic recovery have given way to governments embarking on separate deep national deficit reduction programmes, each hoping to cut its way to generating the conditions for future growth.

This ascendancy of the right both reflects and represents the political failure of Europe's left. But the crisis of Europe's left does not have a single cause – indeed it has many dimensions.

The triple crises of Europe's left

A crisis of political support
The political crisis is not simply a matter of the centre-left having lost national elections in one country after another. That there are now inquests taking place after election defeats in Britain, Germany, Sweden and the Netherlands, while similar debates have long seemed to be in

1

permanent session in France, Italy and Poland, suggests that attributing national explanations can only form part of the story. The failure of other governments, and the swing of the political pendulum, can bring centre-left parties to power, sometimes in the most thankless of circumstances – as in Greece and perhaps shortly in Ireland too. But this is not the same as having an alternative agenda. And even those centre-left parties which have been successfully re-elected, in Spain and Portugal, also now face deep challenges of renewal which their sister parties in power failed to resolve.

Underpinning electoral failure is a deeper crisis of political representation. The social impacts of economic change, and questions of identity, welfare and immigration, risk creating new cleavages within the electoral coalitions that the centre-left would need to keep together in order to govern. The ability to govern from the left-of-centre has always depended on an ability to construct cross-class coalitions within our societies. At the root of the social democratic dilemma is the question of whether and how this is still possible.

A crisis of political economy

The financial crash of 2008 offered an important opportunity to rebalance debates about political economy. "The economic crisis was not caused by government. It was caused by the lack of government" and so presented "a moment of profound crisis for the idea that the answer as far as possible is to leave the market to its own devices", as Ed Miliband (then Climate Change Secretary in the British government) told the Fabian New Year Conference in January 2009. That perception was accurately reflected in the hands-on response of governments of every political perspective to the immediate crisis. Yet the crisis also profoundly challenged the social democratic settlement on political economy of the 1990s, in which globalisation was not simply accepted as inevitable, but liberal political economy and finance-led growth were championed as the means of resourcing social democratic ambitions for public spending and redistribution. Social democracy's mission was never to end capitalism but to tame and manage it; social democracy is nothing without a political economy to create the more sustainable capitalism it wants.

A crisis of multilateral legitimacy
The political dilemmas of social democracy may be sharpest of all when it comes to the politics of international co-operation, perhaps now both more necessary and more difficult than ever. There is no viable project for 'social democracy in one country', simply because no effective political project for a fairer, more secure and more sustainable society will be possible anywhere in our continent by thinking only within national boundaries. Yet if citizens are disconnected from national politicians and parties, seeing them as an elite and out-of-touch professional cadre, how much more disconnected are they from the complex labyrinth of overlapping multilateralisms, both in the European Union and beyond it?

A decade of constitutional debate in the European Union, intended to reconnect the EU with its citizens, did more to exacerbate these problems than to resolve them. Any social democratic project must address this disconnection, but any sense that this seeks to impose a global social democracy from above will simply reinforce a feeling that social democracy has lost touch with what people want.

Refoundations

What endures in social democracy
The need for a refounding of the European centre-left – a 'new generation' – is now a common theme and shared point of departure in political debates across the continent. So each party is engaged in a significant re-examination – in civic debate beyond the parties – of not just its policies,

but its ideas, its organisation and culture, and strategies for mobilising political support. There are also valuable efforts within the Party of European Socialists and the FEPS 'Next Left' project to link these European debates.

A common starting point in these debates is that they must entail a rethinking on at least the same scale as the 1990s, which created a generational shift across the European centre-left through the creation of New Labour and other competing varieties of 'third way' social democracy [as Alfred Gusenbauer argues in Chapter 3]; and perhaps the most profound process of political renewal since the German Social Democrats' revisionist shift away from Marxism at Bad Godesberg in 1959, which set out the contours for social democracy in the era of Europe's golden age.

But we should resist the idea that the era of European social democracy has come to a full stop, and has little to offer beyond a lament for a 'better yesterday'. Rumours of the death of European social democracy are much exaggerated. Indeed, part of the crisis of social democratic identity is that the values, historic institutional achievements and contemporary goals of social democracy have now become the common terrain of European politics. A refounding of social democracy should be rooted in a recognition of how its own enduring values provide important strengths for a renewal of Europe's left.

The triumph of social democratic values

The *values* of social democracy have triumphed, at least; they are deeply embedded in most European societies. What is striking during this moment of political gloom for the centre-left is that its core goals are now much less politically contested by the political right than they were a generation ago. Where the centre-right has succeeded electorally, it has often done so through the theft of social democratic rhetoric, staking a claim to be better protectors and champions of left values than the social democrats. Fredrik Reinfeldt was re-elected in Sweden on the claim that the right were "the real guarantors of the welfare state". While Margaret Thatcher came to bury socialism in Britain, David Cameron praises the social mission of the left. Thatcher explicitly made a public case for greater inequality ("let our children grow tall – and some of them taller than others if they have it in themselves to do so"), David Cameron pledges that his party is better placed to achieve 'progressive ends' of reducing poverty and inequality, albeit through the 'conservative means' of shrinking the state.

Across the political spectrum, populist left parties present themselves as champions of authentic left values, while even right populists articulate their grievances in the name of fairness and often make a defence of social provision part of their cultural identity politics.

The persistence of social democratic institutions

For three decades, one of the most vocal public arguments has been that the social democratic achievement of collective welfare provision would be unaffordable and unsustainable in the global era. That Finland and Sweden top global competitiveness league tables shows the evidence is weak. But the real reason why so much state welfare spending survived everywhere in the neoliberal era is that citizens did not want to slash it.

The current austerity crisis offers a new moment of opportunity which the minimal state right is eager to seize in many European countries. Yet achieving this ideological ambition depends entirely on denying that it exists, with liberal, centre-right and right-wing parties at pains to present cuts as only a necessary and regrettable response to circumstances, though the evidence is of rather more mixed motives than that.

The spread of social democratic internationalism

Multilateral international co-operation is not a theory but a fact of life. The *sui generis* nature of the European Union once seemed primarily a reflection of the distinctive historic experience of Europe's 20th century. Increasingly, it plays a part in an overlapping network of multilateral co-operation in which politics and power in global forums have an increasingly European feel, where sovereignty has meaning as a voice and seat at the table in resolving major global challenges.

Every government – whether led by social democrats, Christian Democrats or the neo-conservatives of the Bush administration – could suddenly see the case for the necessary role of government intervention. Today, even Conservative Eurosceptics like British Foreign Secretary William Hague find themselves making the case for constructive engagement in the European Union – pursuing deeper Anglo-French defence co-operation, making the case for British participation in EU, supporting an Irish 'bailout' and supporting modest German proposals for treaty revisions. Britain's deep political divisions over whether to be part of the EU at all – which hobbled prime ministers and chancellors, and pitched political parties into civil war – may yet be fizzling out, not with a bang but a whimper. If we have yet to resolve the democratic dilemmas of multilateral co-operation, nobody doubts that multilateral co-operation is here to stay.

Taking the long view, the contemporary crisis of Europe's left is one born of political success as well as failure. It is the right's convergence on the rhetoric and practice of social democracy which has created a crisis of social democratic identity. But though the historic achievements of social democracy remain popular, the vision of the better society of the future is opaque, and the politics of securing support to make it possible are daunting.

The parties of 'no'?

Being out of power across most of Europe presents an opportunity for the left to primarily focus on articulating anger and opposition to whatever governments propose. This can be electorally successful. The US Republicans were criticized for being 'the party of 'no'', lacking a constructive argument as they made sweeping gains in the 2010 US mid-term elections, fuelled by the rejectionist energy of populist Tea Party campaigns. Similar energies have brought some electoral success to European populists of left and right, often able to offer a more visceral, emotional and apparently authentic connection to the grievances of particular groups. Deep public spending cuts are sparking a new era of political protest, and are politicising a generation fearful that they will bear the brunt of a crisis they did little to create.

The centre-left has been less effective than the political right in understanding the emotional as well as the rational content of politics. After every national political defeat, former ministers talked about how parties in government became too technocratic and policy-focused, easily perceived as a new establishment rather than an insurgent political force.

So perhaps social democracy in the 1990s at times involved too much head and not enough heart. But using the opportunity of opposition to choose a politics which is all heart and no head is unlikely to be the answer. Unlike Europe's populist parties – or indeed US Congressmen – a social democratic left must be able to offer a constructive governing project.

Left politics must engage with and seek to lead and articulate political opposition and protest. But anger is unlikely to prove a sustainable political motivation; the task of social democracy is to turn this into pressure for possible alternatives.

Signposts towards the next left

1. More ideology on values; more pluralism in organisation

The starting point for social democratic renewal is to show how parties can become more ideologically rooted in clear values and principles while being decisively more pluralist and open in the way they operate politically.

This is a challenge to the conventional orthodoxy, that ideology and values weigh modern parties down. The loosening of political allegiances has seen parties refashion themselves as 'catch all' parties, able to appeal across society. If the right had to talk about inequality, the left's priority was to show that it had come to terms with the market. Social democrats have been sometimes less confident than their opponents in articulating social democratic values, for fear that a 'retreat' to a more ideological social democracy would be a recipe for defeat, appealing to a shrinking electoral and social base.

Every party faces a more pluralist political environment than half a century ago. They should engage with environmentalism, to ensure that a new social democracy combines the best of red and green thinking. While parties naturally focus on winning elections, they need to see themselves as part of broader advocacy movements, shifting the attitudes and context within which elections take place. This will demand a significant shift in the culture and organisation of party politics. Social democracy needs to be more confident that it is rooted in its own political values if it is to make common cause with movements and allies outside political parties, and successfully engage with a more plural political environment.

2. The fairness contract: the politics of a progressive majority

It has to remain the social democratic ambition to pursue

both economic prosperity and social justice, along with a greater awareness of the limits of environmental sustainability. The argument with the modern centre-right is in rejecting the Panglossian claim that no trade-offs are necessary to achieve this. The social democracy of the 1990s did make the case for interventions in the market – as with New Labour introducing the minimum wage in Britain – but, as both David Coats and Roger Liddle set out here, it was slow to recognise and respond to the scale of insecurities created by contemporary capitalism. The distinctive social democratic argument is that fairness doesn't happen by chance. By claiming the rhetoric of social democracy while decrying social democratic means, centre-right governments set themselves a 'fairness test' which they appear likely to fail.

The core mission of social democracy has the potential to remain more robust in more diverse societies than many fear. There is no hard evidence to support the thesis that increased diversity is incompatible with the desire to contribute to the collective pot. But tensions around immigration and identity can play an important role in exacerbating existing 'fairness' grievances about the fairness and reciprocity of welfare, and social democrats must address this in order to sustain majority support. This is demonstrated by the experience of Britain in the last decade. There had been a sharp retrenchment of the public sector in the 1980s. Britain after 2000 was more diverse – but that did not prevent growing pressure for more public spending (and grudging support for the tax to pay for it) when it came to spending on the NHS, education and redistribution through tax credits for those in work.

These areas of public spending were not vulnerable to a 'them and us' grievance politics between contributors and recipients about who deserved what. Where that was the case – in social housing and unemployment benefits – it was much harder to spend more. The issue is not about diversity itself, but about the institutional strategies of welfare design – universal structures, which reflect contribution as well as need. This demands a social democratic politics for a fairer and more equal society – and a strategy which pursues routes to reduce inequality that chime with fairness attitudes rather than challenge them.

A central western narrative has been that the rise of China and India will create a 'race to the bottom', as developing countries compete on wages and labour conditions. But a theme of the next twenty years will be the emergence of a Chinese welfare state, or what the Government calls a "welfare society with Chinese characteristics"; a government-commissioned expert panel has proposed a blueprint to expand its fledgling safety net to provide universal healthcare, pensions, unemployment insurance and minimum living allowances by 2049. (This half-tribute to social democracy is not yet, regrettably, accompanied by parallel progress on the democracy track). That is partly a necessary response to China's ageing society, which shows how predictions that European demographics will mean the end of unaffordable European welfare miss the mark. A retreat from collective provision will not offer any solution to growing demands for social care. All parties will be engaged in an argument about the recasting of contributory welfare models, not their abandonment, so another central social challenge of our age is again likely to be conducted on primarily social democratic terrain.

3. Social democracy from the bottom to the top: a new politics of multilateralism

All politics is local – and all politics is global too. The new social democracy can be created in the space which seeks to connect these competing truths.

It is in national and local politics that each European social democratic party must secure the trust and support needed to govern, articulating the hopes, fears and aspirations of its own society, and responding primarily to the pressures of a national political cycle. There are many common issues: opportunity and insecurity, fairness and inequality, identity and integration. Yet the way in which we apply similar values to these issues will often have distinctive features – reflecting national discourses of citizenship and identity; different pathways in the design of welfare institutions; and overlapping but nationally rooted traditions of our parties and movements.

So the task of a shared social democratic project needs to respect and reflect these differences, *and* recognise the contemporary limits of any project that attempts to go it alone. We cannot think we can exert democratic choice over the forces shaping our lives only in our local street, the town hall or even the national parliament.

Many national parties are now engaged in a necessary process of *relocalisation*, to re-engage with the communities they seek to serve, to re-learn how to organise on the ground, as well as to adopt new methods of organisation in the internet age. The proof that social democrats should never have let themselves become caricatured as distant, elite parties most comfortable in the institutions of the state can be found in their own histories, which often contained powerful, though sometimes neglected traditions, of mutualism and civic engagement. The left which achieved the European welfare model was, in many ways, different from that which has lived off it – it now needs to re-learn the lesson of how it won the argument which allowed it to reshape the state and society in the first place.

The only way to create effective European and global responses will be to demonstrate that parties and governments are responding to democratic *pressure from below* for action on jobs and growth, financial reform, climate change and development. The incremental development of pan-European party co-operation is important, in helping to establish that we do share a common frame of values, even if we cannot expect to quickly resolve all of the policy differences in a common manifesto. What would help to create a left-right politics at the European level would be to carefully select some key battles – choosing causes, whether taxing banks or action on the climate – which we must tackle together, so that national parties and activists might engage not from a sense of duty, but because it actively adds to our campaigning on the ground.

Making a new case for Europe
This should change the way we talk about Europe too. Europe was a great cause for the political generations who constructed it, or who led their national debates to 'join Europe', in Britain and Scandinavia in the 1970s, southern Europe in the 1980s and in central and Eastern Europe after 1989. The expectation of 'founding' generations that those who followed would be 'natural Europeans' was not fulfilled, except perhaps that we can take the significant historic achievements of the EU largely for granted.

We may be deeply engaged with internationalist causes, but these will usually seem very disconnected from the complex institutional labyrinth of European politics to anybody outside the professional political classes. The traditional arguments for the EU and European integration (and perhaps those against them as well) may resonate much less for a generation for whom the first cultural image thrown up by the idea of 'Europe' is more likely to be the Champions League than the Second World War, or even the fall of the Berlin Wall.

But we might learn something for our politics from this shared European experience of the Champions League. Champions League Europe reflects the transformation of Europe's football clubs by migration across the continent and around the world, yet they remain the focus of intense local pride, community and identity.

The clubs compete at national and European level, after proposals that they exit national football to create a 'European super league' were rejected as they lacked public legitimacy. The matches, played simultaneously around Europe, are the single largest shared continental experience which Europeans enjoy together. Yet, beyond a small cosmopolitan elite, the sports pages and TV coverage primarily focuses on the national club's participation in the shared European space, until the final approaches.

European football offers a policy laboratory of different approaches. FC Barcelona – a supporter-owned mutualist co-operative – plays against PLCs and private companies purchased with leveraged debt. Different national priorities are reflected in domestic regulation – with Germany paying more attention to the interests of its national team than the English, while trading-off the ability to maximise income to keep free-to-air TV broadcasting and lower ticket prices. But there is ongoing discussion too about the Europe-wide rules needed to maintain a fair level playing field. New European-wide 'financial fair play' regulations will be introduced, ending unfair competition through billionaire oligarchs and to prevent a bubble economy imploding in football.

The political lesson to pro-Europeans is to earn permission for the multilateralism we need. The British have a reputation as reluctant Europeans. New YouGov polling commissioned for this book shows why this is, yet it also shows how the British are now very moderate Eurosceptics, with majorities perfectly open to deeper integration wherever it makes sense.

So 45 per cent of British people think the European Union is a bad thing for Britain, and 49 per cent want looser co-operation between European nations. But not everywhere all of the time. Even the rather EU-agnostic British public is ready to accept the case for closer co-operation on climate change, terrorism and diplomacy. There is strong support for minimum EU rights to ensure workers are not undercut by free movement of labour, and there is even support for common business rates. This helps to explain why challenges from sceptics to the current Government's pragmatic engagement in the EU have lacked resonance. Earning permission for necessary integration will succeed as long as the EU can show it will be effective. If these arguments can be won in Britain they can be won everywhere in the EU. Perhaps we have now passed the high tide of Euroscepticism.

* * *

There is no guarantee of a social democratic revival. Social democrats have never believed in a politics of inevitability. Political projects which claim their triumph is pre-ordained are dangerous, disempowering and liable to be disproved by events, as the predictive failure of Marxism and the more recent hubris of neo-conservatism have shown.

But we should have confidence that political progress is possible. If we are convinced that the insecurities of our society require social democratic answers now more than ever, then all that prevents us from doing it is the task of persuading our fellow citizens that our cause should be their cause too.

2. Inclusive growth: a new European mission for social democracy

Roger Liddle

To say that social democracy is in crisis across Europe is a statement of the obvious. In the late 1990s, an astonishing 13 out of the then EU15 countries had social democrats in government. Those halycon days are long gone as social democratic parties are recording some of their worst results in their history. French Socialists and Danish Social Democrats have not won elections since 1997 and 1998. In 2009, 23 per cent for the German Social Democrats marked their worst ever post-war vote. In 2010, Dutch Labour polled just 20 per cent in a fragmented political scene, the Swedish Social Democrats recorded their worst result since universal suffrage in the 1923, while Labour's second worst performance in the same period was worsted only by the horror of 1983.

One of the biggest challenges for the centre-left across Europe is the increasing levels of insecurity and cultural unease towards migrant communities, reflected in the rise of populist right-wing and anti-immigration parties. It is not only social democrats, but all mainstream parties that have suffered to some extent from this rise in populism. Yet it is European social democracy that is in existential crisis. Many cite organisational decline as a root cause: falls in party membership, the diminishing position of trade unions, and the centre-left's disadvantage in funding election campaigns are not unique to Britain. Yet these are symptoms not causes. Far more serious is a lack of clarity of purpose. In *Southern Discomfort Again*, Policy Network's analysis of the 2010 general election result, only 37 per cent of UK voters in the south and Midlands were clear what Labour now stood for. A similar story can be told across Europe.

What is to be done? The example of New Labour continues to fascinate European social democrats, but there is a real risk that the discussion so far ignores the long term structural factors in New Labour's decline. Social democracy needs a radical rethinking of its approach to the welfare state, a new political economy, and a deeper recognition of the limits of nation-state social democracy. The European Union has a central role to play in social democratic strategy and policy.

The real reasons behind New Labour's decline

Long-running structural factors are crucial in explaining the weakening of social democracy since the mid-1990s. These are far more important than the superficial froth of Blair-Brown rivalries, so prominent in contemporary memoirs and accounts, or the impact of the war in Iraq, though this did significantly weaken Labour's hold over 'progressive' opinion, particularly in the media and among intellectuals.

Of these structural factors, the most important is the impact of globalisation: in polarising market outcomes between winners and losers, resulting in the declining fortunes of the low skilled in the labour market; in the 'hollowing out' of decent jobs in the middle; and the acceleration of rewards at the very top to a degree that few anticipated. The increased importance of education in a knowledge and service economy widened opportunities for many, but heightened divisions between those who got to university and those who did not. This is the root of the alienation of the 'squeezed middle'. For all the media's sneering at this concept, it is a fact that pre-tax earnings for workers whose wages are around the median of the wage distribution, rose slowly in real terms from 2005, if at all, whereas earnings growth had been buoyant in the earlier Blair years.

So it is not surprising that migration was perceived by many as a threat to wages and family living standards, and as weakening traditional ties of solidarity, though other longer term factors such as the decline of community and the rise of individualism had also been corrosive. The pace of welfare state reform was too slow in responding to the changing nature of the labour market and the family, and the new social risks people face. The unacceptably high persistence of worklessness among people of working age gravely undermined the perception of fairness which is the welfare state's vital underpinning. All these factors added to the widespread alienation from Labour of the 'squeezed middle', gnawing away at the foundations of the New Labour 'big tent' that Tony Blair had so skilfully erected in the 1990s.

The welfare state needs much more than a post-Beveridge patch-up. Social and economic change makes a fundamental rethink inevitable. The impact of globalisation and technology on the labour market has been to reverse the shift in the balance of power that characterised the post-war years. We need much more than nostalgia for a more comfortable past to work out how the present realities of free capital mobility, ever more rapid technological change and mass migration can be managed to produce better quality job opportunities and a more favourable income distribution for the bottom half of the workforce. The 'third way' response of better equipping people for change through investment in human capital and active labour market policies is clearly not a sufficient answer to the dilemma, even it remains a necessary one. The state needs to take a stronger developmental role through a more activist industrial policy in shaping labour market outcomes and increasing employer demand for better quality jobs.

At the same time the welfare state faces new costly demands – not just greater life expectancy, and more frail and vulnerable people among the elderly, but also new

social risks of poverty such as the prevalence of relationship breakdown or the redundancy of skills that now can
be overtaken in mid career by technological advance.
These challenges of changing demography and new social
risks are probably on a greater scale than the cost of the
long term fiscal adjustment we face in the wake of the 2008
banking crisis.

Secondly, without radical innovation in the way public
services are delivered, the rising costs of highly labour
intensive activities will become an unsupportable drag on
future welfare state sustainability. The Achilles heel of the
Nordic model could well be that rising demand and costs
come up against a tax constraint, forcing a rethink of traditional notions of entitlement and universality.

Thirdly, if Europe is serious about tackling climate
change, there appears no alternative to much higher energy
prices and huge lifestyle change. This challenges the mate-
rialism of the traditional social democratic attachment to
better living standards for working people, particularly
threatening to middle income families who have fled the
cities for the freedoms and security of new outer suburbs
and country towns, and a car-dependent way of life.

If social democracy is to recommit to a new offer of
security for all through a re-energised welfare state, it
must find acceptable solutions to these objective realities.
It has to define a new concept of fairness that will stand
the test of public acceptability in a more fractured, diverse
and individualistic society where the public discourse is
dominated by tales of scroungers, welfare cheats and
migrants jumping the queue. For social democrats to be
crystal clear what they think is fair and unfair is not to
bend the knee to media driven right wing fantasies. It is
essential if popular support for a modern welfare state is
to be rebuilt. Bill Clinton recognised this truth with his
notorious soundbite that he would "end welfare as we
know it". The welfare reforms Congress eventually imple-
mented were harsher than Clinton himself would have

wanted because they had to be negotiated with Republican Congressional leadership. But a big regret about the New Labour years is that Labour did promise to "think the unthinkable" about the welfare state and then, notwithstanding occasional flurries of bold reform from some individual ministers, backed away from any consistent reform strategy. Now that in Britain the Conservative-Liberal Democrat coalition is pressing ahead with welfare reforms led by the former Conservative leader, Iain Duncan Smith, it would be politically easy – but a mistake – for Labour simply to condemn what is proposed. Douglas Alexander, Labour's new shadow spokesperson deserves credit for not following that mistaken course. The challenge for Labour is to advocate a financially viable alternative reform strategy that it can argue is genuinely fairer.

This is all a far cry from the massive enthusiasm that Tony Blair generated as newly elected Labour leader in the mid-1990s. The temptation now on the critical left is to dismiss Blair as a crypto-Tory who only made Labour safe and electable by compromising with the right. Nothing could be further from the truth. In the 1990s, Blair inspired the highest of progressive hopes and made millions look at Labour afresh, presenting a morally appealing and bold vision for reform of his country that rested on a commitment to renew the public realm. Its practical expression was a promised transformation of public services: "my priority is education, education, education" and a commitment to "save the NHS".

At one level Labour substantially delivered on this pledge. It had a proud record of achievement in raising standards in education, health and other public services and widening choice for those who could never afford to 'go private', and tackling child and pensioner poverty. However, there was no compelling narrative of social justice to offset the steady chipping away of support that the daily grind of government brings. Rather the reverse was true. Labour alienated potential support with what the historians, David Marquand and Peter Clarke, have described as a "mechanical" rather than "moral" approach to reform. New Labour in government pushed and pulled at the Whitehall levers which its parliamentary majorities at Westminster supposedly gave its ministers control over. It is unfair to portray Labour treating the British public services rather in the way Gosplan hoped to transform the Soviet economy, but there is enough of a grain of truth to make the charge damaging.

Labour ministers took up the nostrums of new public management theory that had gained sway under the Thatcher era and made them Labour's own. The whole paraphernalia of 'delivery' – with its profusion of top down targets, service standards, quasi-markets, independent regulators, multi area agreements, specific grants and incentives and 'earned autonomy', took faith in managerialism, presumed benevolent by being better incentivised and regulated, to a new and higher level. This was all for the best of motives, but ended up being counterproductive. Instead of transforming the dedication of public employees into ever more 'knightly' efforts on behalf of the public they serve (in a typology that the LSE's Julian Le Grand invented), it encouraged the mentality of the 'knave' in ticking boxes, playing by the rules and working the system. One of the most striking and depressing conclusions of the *Southern Discomfort Again* analysis is that in the 2010 election, nearly half swing voters concluded that the additional billions Labour spent on public services were frittered away in bureaucracy and waste. The correct conclusion is not that New Labour failed to reform enough; but that the methods it chose failed to mobilise public opinion, still less build any kind of popular movement, for a fairer, more decent society.

This was a striking contrast to New Labour in the 1990s. While Tony Blair is now remembered particularly for persuading Labour to come to terms with the market economy through the re-writing of Clause IV,,it is forgotten that in arguing this, he expressed his real convictions in terms of solidarity, partnership and community. Unlike Margaret Thatcher he stood for something called 'society' as against the creeping reach of doctrinal neo liberalism. But despite the pre-1997 eloquence of his belief in 'community', in government very little happened to translate those high ideals into practice.

The extent of this failure is brought home by David Cameron's success today in stealing the New Labour language of community and promoting the concept of the 'Big Society' as his big idea. This is why the old internal Labour debate about the merits of 'public service reform' is off target. The so-called Blairite insistence on market driven 'reform' is as much a narrow a cul-de-sac as so-called Brownite 'statism'. Labour would do much better to embrace the precepts of the "Big Society" and argue for genuine diversity of public service provision and the promotion of new forms of provider such as not for profit providers, mutuals and cooperatives. This would enable Labour to question the opening up of the public service marketplace to big private company providers which is what many of the interests backing the Conservatives are aiming for. Labour could then develop policies to explain how in what would be a new, more diverse public sector landscape, it would pursue the social democratic objective of more equal access to the highest standards for all.

The need for a new social democratic political economy

It is becoming commonplace to say that the problem with New Labour's political economy in the last decade and a half is that it acquiesced too readily in the ideological triumph of the Anglo American model of capitalism, particularly the deregulation of financial markets. Having broken with Labour's statist past, Tony Blair and Gordon Brown proved unable to strike the right new balance between the market and the state. Their failure to do so was based on twin assumptions that proved to be flawed. On the one hand, the sympathy of big business was seen a crucial test of economic 'competence' and electability. On the other, the centre-left's politics of redistribution depended on the tax revenues that market-driven deregulated growth would bring. The weakness of New Labour's reliance on business endorsement was exposed in the 2010 election campaign, when top business leaders backed Conservative plans for sharper cuts in public spending and to reverse Labour's planned rise in National Insurance contributions. At the same time the crisis in UK public finances exposed the fragility of Britain's tax revenues and their overdependence on the City of London and an unsustainable bubble in bank lending. Together these factors gravely weakened Labour's economic credibility. And they exposed Labour politically for having acquiesced in a culture of reward, especially in financial services, that was an affront to the public's values of fairness, enabling Labour's opponents to walk away with the mantle of social justice for themselves.

I believed strongly – and still do believe – that social democracy has to work closely in partnership with business. But it is a responsible form of capitalism that social democrats ought to foster, not singing hymns of praise to deregulated financial markets, where both Brown and Blair were equally at fault. Of course a flourishing entrepreneurial and innovative culture requires an acceptance of incentives and an avoidance of penal taxation, but it does not mean that wealth, *however gained*, is legitimate. The 2008 crisis has reminded us that what happened was far more than technical failure of regulation: unregulated capitalism with the wrong values can result in catastrophic market failure. In 2008 Gordon Brown to his credit recognised that there had to be change, even though in its attitudes to the banks after the crisis, the Labour Government often looked uncertain as to which way to turn, perhaps understandably given the huge conflict of objectives it then faced. But Tony Blair appears from his memoirs even to reject the necessary adjustment to New Labour thinking that Gordon Brown and Peter Mandelson made after 2008.

Across Europe, the centre-left needs to come to terms with an uncomfortable truth: that it has lost out to the centre-right during the global financial crisis. The crisis has been redefined successfully by the right within the space of two years as a crisis of government deficits, rising public debt and a failing Euro. The right have convinced the public that culpability lies in the inefficiency of the state, not the inherent instability of inadequately regulated markets. Ironically, this should have been a uniquely social democratic moment; in truth, however, the crisis showed the guiding assumptions of the centre-left's politics and governing model to be shattered. To regain power across Europe, we must focus on repairing these foundations.

The political and policy challenge for social democrats is to build a 'new European model of capitalism'. In essence the driver of this new model remains the goal of robust economic growth – but an 'inclusive growth' that in contrast to the past two decades is socially fairer, benefits all regions, results in less inequality, delivers more and better quality jobs, is more environmentally sustainable, and more concerned with improving citizens' quality of life and less with crude measures of GDP. This is a tall order. There may be contradictions and trade offs to resolve. But social democracy is not worth much if it lacks ambition.

The centrality of a European perspective

This new model capitalism can only be built if social democrats accept that the European Union in which we share a common destiny as partners becomes a vital dimension of our politics. In Britain, although the vast majority of Labour Party members are now instinctively pro-European, we have yet to incorporate the reality of the EU into our politics and our way of thinking. In the recent leadership election, none of the candidates presented a positive programme for the EU, not even as an optional add-on, though it has to be a central part of their political mission.

The reason of course is that voters in Britain – and increasingly in other parts of the EU ¬– don't like the EU very much. And this is even truer of many newspaper outlets who determine our parties' ability to get our general political message across to the public. So we push to the back of our minds the enormous practical significance of our EU membership. For example in Britain we neglect to explain to our supporters that the UK economy is wholly integrated into the European Single Market and that any growth policy for Britain will only work properly if there is a complementary growth policy in the rest of Europe, and especially the Euro area with which our economic future is bound. The present conjuncture of each member state outdoing each other in stringency in order to gain competitive advantage for a bigger share of sluggish EU growth is doomed to failure.

Labour talks of building a new economic model for Britain, but if we want tighter financial regulation and new corporate governance rules, what happens at EU level is crucial. Similarly, in order to best protect our welfare state from spending cuts in this age of austerity, the social democratic capacity to raise taxation without running the risk of a flight of companies overseas could be greatly enhanced by tax coordination at EU level. New tax revenues can be found by the introduction of EU wide taxes on carbon consumption and financial transactions, which would be ineffective or self-destructive on a purely national basis. If we are serous about managing migration, we have a self interest in promoting growth through the Structural Funds in the dismally poor – and getting poorer – regions of the EU whose citizens want to leave. In addition how migration controls are enforced at the EU common border should be of great British concern.

The problem is that we still play politics as if it is still a wholly national game. And of course by exaggerating what nation states can do, and underplaying how important in reality the EU now is in shaping the possibilities of politics, in the long run we do politics itself, and our own legitimacy with the voters, a great disservice. This matters a lot less for the Conservatives in Britain because they position themselves as sceptics about Europe anyway. But Labour takes both the electoral hit for being pro-Europe and fails to demonstrate how a positive social democratic policy for the EU can be constructed. Europe has to be a vital component of social democracy's way forward.

The traditional nation-state conception of social democracy is at the end of the road. Social democrats must finally come to terms with the new reality that 'all politics is global'. While many social democrats recognised interdependence, fought hard for international development and emphasised the new importance of climate change, they failed to come to terms with the full domestic impact of globalisation, destroying good quality traditional working class jobs, as sector after sector is forced to adjust to Asian competition. Instead we argued that the only role for government was to 'equip people for change'. Of course there is a lot of truth in this – and active policies for education, skills and modernising welfare are crucial. However social democrats failed to develop at EU level a proper strategy for globalisation.

A successful European social democratic programme has to focus on rebuilding a sense of solid mutual interest between member states. High sounding appeals to European solidarity may go down well in left wing European gatherings, but they cut little ice with today's public. The pragmatic European social democrat cannot simply deplore the mindset of German workers whose standard of living has been squeezed in order to facilitate German recovery and are not minded to see their hard-earned taxes subsidising what they imagine to be featherbedded or feckless cheats in other member states. And it is no use blaming the populism of the media for ordinary people's narrow-mindedness. Politically it is as pointless as complaining about the weather.

Much can only be achieved by our national parties winning national elections, pressing on with economic and social reforms that reflect national specificities. But my argument is that a *necessary* condition of success in a highly interdependent European economy is for social democrats in government in member states to share a common vision, in which the development of particular EU policies plays an *essential* supporting and conditioning role. So building a new European model of capitalism is also about resolving the EU's current crisis of political stagnation and legitimacy.

A social democratic plan for European recovery and inclusive growth

The medium term position in Europe looks bad. The southern mediterranean member states and Ireland are locked in what looks a long lasting triple vice of austerity. For them there is no alternative to sustained deficit reduction – despite the negative consequences for growth. Appeasing bond market fears of debt sustainability has to come first. And the pain of gradual disinflation to restore their competitiveness within the Eurozone – through an 'internal devaluation' of relative cuts in the real value of wages and social benefits – could go on for years. A decade of high unemployment and social tension is in prospect.

Indeed, across the EU as a whole, the consequences of the 2008 banking crisis are serious and long-lasting and have put new barriers in the way of growth. The private sector banks' reduced appetite for risk will mean less finance for new and growing businesses or big risky projects. At the same time the requirements of fiscal consolidation will constrain social ambitions. This is not an optimistic setting for our politics and the overhang of deficit reduction will cast a long shadow, as Europe this decade has also to come to terms with public finance consequences of its ageing demography.

The best that can be said for the EU response so far is that it has just about coped: the member state-led bank rescue and coordinated fiscal stimulus in 2008; the IMF led rescue package for Greece in 2010; the Commission's proposals for an unavoidable strengthening of EU level financial regulation; and the Eurogroup proposals for improved economic governance and a new crisis resolution mechanism. For EU institutionalists, these responses represent a significant deepening of economic integration. In a sense they are right, as stronger EU rules for financial regulation, fiscal discipline, crisis management and member state debt restructuring are the likely end result. But it all has the flavour either of 'shutting the stable door after the horse has bolted', or coping better with future disasters, rather than the forward looking policy Europe needs to put its economy in a better place.

European social democracy must become the credible advocate of a more growth-oriented macro-economic framework for Europe. Because economic interdependence is far greater than it was three decades ago, the question of how best to renew growth is an unavoidable 'common concern'. Social democrats now have to start saying this loud and clear. However, for this to go beyond platitudes, winning German acceptance for growth-oriented reforms to governance of the Euro is essential. High public sector deficits are justifiable temporarily on legitimate Keynesian anti-recessionary grounds. But were social democrats to imply that they are permanently not a problem, it would be a recipe for economic irrelevance and political impotence.

First, social democrats should argue for a new grand bargain in Europe: tougher binding rules on unacceptably high public sector deficits, in exchange for new obligations to boost domestic demand for member states running high external surpluses. Technocratically this means comparative national competitiveness must become a European issue alongside public sector debts and deficits. Politically however this involves a big step: the Europeanisation of debate about wages and salaries. The principal reason that the southern member states are in trouble in the Euro single currency bloc is not that they lack the freedom to devalue, but that wages and salaries have run ahead of productivity. In Germany on the other hand, the profit share in national income has risen as the wage share has declined. At the same time unfair wage competition is seen in parts of the EU15 as driving down wages at the bottom end – as a result of capital mobility within the enlarged single market and economic migration from the poorer member states.

Wage competition from central and eastern Europe is inevitable and legitimate as the principal driver of catch-up growth, yet it needs to be managed in a mutually acceptable way. Economists are right that labour migration is a key tool of adjustment. But this can only be made acceptable with a new balance of policy that enhances EU migrants' social rights and at the same time allays fears of 'social dumping'. A political pushback against recent European Court of Justice judgements could be achieved through a revision of the Posting of Workers Directive, that requires a member state's minimum terms and conditions to apply to workers posted temporarily from another country to work in that state. This raises difficult issues, but should be part of a balanced package, as should a commitment to sustain Structural Fund transfers to economically weak regions despite EU budgetary pressures. To be acceptable to taxpayers in the 'net paying' member states, much stronger conditionality in relation to good governance needs to be attached.

If social democrats are to develop a common agenda for economic recovery and inclusive growth, then wage coordination between member states, minimum wages within member states, new and fairer forms of profit sharing, action against unacceptable 'social dumping', and regional transfers all have to be part of it.

Secondly, social democracy has to identify and foster new drivers of sustainable green growth that will be of benefit across the continent. Europe must become the global exemplar of low carbon transition and green growth. This presents both a social challenge and a massive economic opportunity. The challenge is to manage the decarbonisation of Europe's heavy industries, for which the Schuman plan that founded the Coal and Steel Community in the 1950s provides a model. The opportunity lies in the investment demand that the necessary modernisation and reconfiguration of Europe's energy and transport infrastructure will generate. Getting the economic, regulatory and financing frameworks right at EU level to facilitate large scale private sector investment is essential, but not enough on its own. An EU wide Low Carbon Investment Bank should be spun off from the European Investment Bank, with an innovative facility to raise taxpayer backed Eurobonds for low carbon infrastructures. This would be 'borrowing to invest' for clear and specific infrastructure purposes; not bail outs for member states with unsustainable debt and deficits, but pump priming projects from which the southern and new member states would be important beneficiaries.

Thirdly social democrats should be advocates of policies to stimulate a new wave of private sector-led, commercial innovation at the high-tech knowledge frontier. Too much of the European economy is still attached to a low wage, low skill, 'bargain basement' approach to competitiveness, that in a world of strong Asian competition is a lost cause. Instead the whole of Europe needs to upscale – hence the need for higher public investment in research, modern day skills and supportive digital infrastructures. For all the self-satisfaction in the wake of the 2008 banking crisis that the US model of capitalism had met its come-uppance, 'knowledge' investment in research, higher education, and IT in the EU still massively lags behind the United States. Yet this is the only way for advanced industrial societies that have lost millions of 'good working class jobs' to demonstrate

Europe's social models can survive and prosper in a global-ising economy. New EU initiatives can help: an EU budget reform to transfer wasteful CAP spending on rich farmers to expanded European research and scholarship pro-grammes; 'knowledge investment targets' set for each member state, differentiating between their stages of eco-nomic development; and the new budget deficit rules should take account of 'social investment' in assessing the sustainability of national public finances.

Fourthly, social democrats have to recognise that a rein-vigoration of the single market is the most important EU policy needed to drive a new wave of innovation. All the evidence suggests that far more could be done to open up economic opportunities for dynamic firms, particularly in services, without adopting a dogmatic neoliberalism. But political support for a dynamic single market can only be re-kindled if the fruits of growth are shown to be distrib-uted 'fairly'. Rewards at the top need to be transparent and justifiable; the new European-style capitalism should espouse the business ethics of long-termism over short-ter-mism; and social partnership and stakeholder accountabili-ty over crude ideas of shareholder value. Corporate gover-nance laws should be strengthened to reinforce this. The current state aid rules have sufficient flexibility within them, without destroying their necessary limitations on self destructive competitive subsidies, to permit active govern-ment to play a development role to support new enterprise and strengthen sectoral competitiveness . Reforms on these principles would provide a more supportive socio-econom-ic context for deeper economic integration. They would lib-erate a reinvigorated single market to drive the gains in pro-ductivity and innovation on which Europe's future pros-perity depends.

Fifthly, social democrats should be advocates of a new kind of Social Europe, with a fairer balance between flexibil-ity and security sought at national level appropriate to the circumstances of each member state, but stronger EU tax coordination and an enlarged EU Budget to support vital reforms. We cannot provide economic security by a return to the past. A determined drive for renewed growth through innovation and low carbon transition would represent huge structural change in the EU economy. Labour markets would have to become more effective at promoting adjustment and welfare states need to be modernised – not residualised – to meet the challenges of increasing inequality, embedded disadvantage, ageing populations, and continuing migration. The main impetus for reform has to come from within member states. However all Europe's welfare states depend on an adequate tax base. To safeguard this tax base, social democrats should back a new initiative of fiscal coordination within the EU. After the depredations that tax revenues have suffered in the wake of the global crisis, member states need some protection against destructive tax competition that reduces their capacity to invest in knowledge, infrastructure and welfare state reforms. Without this a 'race to the bottom' on business taxation looms, that could threaten the tax base on which the future of European welfare states depends.

There is also considerable potential for new EU wide taxes that member states cannot effectively levy on their own without inflicting competitive harm on themselves – for example, on financial transactions and carbon emissions. While most of the revenues from such taxes should be returned to member states (to lower taxes and social insurance charges on low paid jobs and thereby boost new job creation), a reformed and expanded EU Budget could help revive the idea of Social Europe. Social democrats should advocate a new social programme at EU level to tackle social disadvantage through the life cycle via an EU framework of objectives, targets, mutual learning and tied Social Fund incentives. Common social objectives could include policies such as: early intervention for disadvantaged children; better child care provision to strengthen the two earner family; the achievement of basic standards of numeracy and literacy and reductions in early school leaving; reversing the decline in social mobility and access to higher education; the need for new entitlements to learning through life; and better management of labour market transitions, especially for the low skilled. This EU framework would not dictate social policy to member states, but it would incentivise progressive national reforms.

Building a new progressive coalition

In the present gloomy moment, some on the left fatalistically believe this is not a time for social democracy. As one former leader of a continental party said to me the other day, "social democrats are not very good at making cuts – so maybe it's a good thing that the right's in charge". But our electorates are not bursting with enthusiasm for the right, as French and German regional elections this year have shown. Politics is open and fluid and social democrats may find themselves winning elections against their own expectations.

So to accept these arguments is a counsel of despair. European societies face several existential threats that should offer social democracy in Europe much needed opportunities for political renewal. These threats all have their origin in the shifting global balance of power.

First, Europe needs to find a sustainable growth model for economic prosperity and social cohesion as a result of the aftershocks of the global economic crisis of 2008, the startling rise of Asia, and the continuing economic weakness of the United States. This must be a more explicitly social democratic version of the EU's Lisbon Agenda of 2000: combining a market liberal drive for faster innovation with more concern for rising inequality, tighter financial regulation, stronger corporate governance reform, and new policies for education, training and the labour market.

Centre-right parties are already trying to move onto to this territory. However they are in hock to financial market orthodoxy and lack a clear strategy for an investment based return to growth within a disciplined fiscal framework. Their fundamental divisions between consensus-minded pragmatic men and women of power and ideologically driven neo-liberal small-staters should create new openings for social democracy.

Secondly, while the immediate pressure for action on climate change has slackened as a result of the recession in the developed world, the pace of Asian expansion will bring the issue back with renewed urgency before long. The only basis for global consensus is that those who have done most to create the problem in the first place must demonstrate the greatest willingness to change their ways. That means principally Europe and the United States, with Europe inevitably forced to take a lead, given the higher level of commitment in Europe to act and the dysfunctionality of US domestic politics. That in turn will provide the basis for a renewal of red-green politics in Europe, as social justice is the only viable long term basis for environmental sustainability. 'Red-green' is a long established formula for the centre-left in many European countries, most notably Germany. But it does not automatically guarantee success. For example in the last Swedish general election, the Social Democrats were damaged by the claim of one prominent Green that no country has proved that it is possible to couple economic growth with responsible natural-resource management. This undermined the capacity of Mona Sahlin's red-green coalition to present a sensible and robust economic policy. Red-green alliances can work but social democrats need a clear strategy in approaching them.

Thirdly, social democrats have the opportunity to make themselves the undisputed champion of European values. The European social model, in all its diversity, is the pinnacle so far of attained of human social achievement. But global power shifts, as well as the growth of religious extremism and violent reactions to Western culture, now make that view seem complacent. To counter this challenge, Europe has to demonstrate new confidence in its values and a new unity of purpose. Internally it requires defeating the politics of race and cultural conflict which define the new populist parties of the right. The mainstream parties of the centre-right are increasingly prisoners of right wing populists, who almost by definition are also deeply hostile to the EU – for example the Wilders party in the Netherlands, the People's Party in Denmark, the Northern League in Italy and even in France, where one of President Sarkozy's main electoral concerns is to suppress any revival of the Le Pennist Front National.

In the United Kingdom, David Cameron's Conservatives now espouse a welcome social liberalism on issues of race. However a deep Euroscepticism has permeated the ranks of the party. It is only Cameron's Whiggish pragmatism, and the necessity he recognised for coalition with the pro-European Liberal Democrats, that keeps the lid, at least for now, on his party's anti-Europeanism. If the centre-right is tempted to embrace populist politics for its own electoral gain, as it may, it will disillusion the centre ground and create new opportunities to build new progressive alliances on the centre and left.

In many countries, politics is fragmenting. As a result, putting together new 'progressive coalitions' appears the only social democratic route back to power. There is certainly merit in this, not least the capacity of such coalitions to re-engage with our disenchanted voters. But social democrats should be wary of quick fixes. Reaching out to left-wing parties, for example, has proved problematic. In Sweden in 2010, 22 per cent of voters who turned away from the Social Democrats blamed their collaboration with the Left Party and 44 per cent viewed the Left has having gained too much influence over social democratic policy. In Germany, attempts by the SPD to forge links with the Die Linke pose similar difficulties. 'Progressive coalitions' may prove successful, but the social democratic element in them has both to be dominant and robust. The compromises involved in embracing green and left wing values can all too easily heighten suspicion among centrist voters about ideological confusion and lack of economic and governing credibility.

That said, an essential task for European social democracy is to build a new pro-European coalition. In European politics, a social democratic programme cannot be exclusively that: to succeed, it has to bring on board Greens and where possible, the less dogmatic anti-globalisers on the left on acceptable terms. It must also build bridges across the centre to social Catholicism and the more responsible and thoughtful elements of the business community. But to do this credibly, social democrats need to be advocates of big new ideas that could capture the public imagination and build confidence in Europe's ability to address its deep problems. Is European social democracy capable of embracing them in contrast to the inertia of the centre-right?

3. The social democratic mission: Lessons from history for the next left

Alfred Gusenbauer

Socialist thought emerged on the European continent in the industrial era.[1] As a 'workers' cause' it quickly became a collective reference point for all those struggling for decent living and working conditions – and it became the practical core of the fight for freedom, justice and equality. These origins define two features of the movement in its early years: association with technological progress on one side, and historical roots primarily in the 'Old Continent' of Europe on the other.

The left goes through ideological turmoil approximately every 50 years. At the turn of the 20th century, this focused on the means of achieving socialism and resulted in a partition between revolutionists (communists) and reformists. A second crisis led to the post-war social democratic settlement, combining a constrained market economy with the modern welfare state. The third moment of turmoil, more recently, has been the attempt to renew social democracy in order to readapt it to the challenges of the 21st century and the era of globalisation. The sentiments that the Third Way aroused are still very vivid across the continent and progressives are still very divided in their assessment of it.

Exploring the ways that the political left responded in these three distinct eras is not just a fascinating theme of historical study – each can also be considered as modernisation agendas for their own times.[2] This evolutionary perspective suggests that any process of renewal that social democracy embarks on now will need to be a long term one. Therefore what is required today should be seen more as a groundbreaking historical change and less as a temporary political fix.

There are several ways that people describe their understanding of social democracy. One could follow the enthusiasts of the essentialist school and embark now on the search for social democracy in terms of restoring our old ideas. This approach tends to be very popular as a sort of post-electoral catharsis when, in the face of a defeat, social democrats jump to the conclusion that they had not been leftist enough before the elections. This may lead to a certain populism that is confident it can detect where the 'political centre' really is.[3] On the other hand it is also the most abused approach by those who habitually rush to proclaim social democracy dead.[4]

The constructive use of our historical inheritance is to seek to use it as a method and resource in designing the contemporary renewal of social democracy. This requires the movement itself to spell out exactly what it is about today. Here it is necessary to provide a distinctive agenda if it is to appear as a coherent force in the eyes of the public. This approach entails a connection between changing operational circumstances and a process of renewal and redefinition.[5] Therefore an understanding of its history is particularly useful while discussing what modern social democracy should be about.

So what are the most important challenges that the 'next left' must respond to? An era of globalisation, post-industrialisation and individualisation: these are the new times that the movement needs to adapt to.

One central consequence of the first challenge – of globalisation – is that a single state alone can no longer determine all its policies and thereby construct the circumstances in which its own population lives. This is due to the global imbedding of markets.[6] These sustain the global dimension of capitalism, which escaped from appropriate regulations and therefore from democratic control. The recent economic and political crisis exposed the vulnerability of such a set up.

Additionally, this is reinforced by two trends that should be central to any discussion about how to reinvent social democracy. The first is that the role of Europe on the world's stage is declining. This is due to a combination of the faster development of the emerging countries, and also to the relative decrease in its GDP and so its actual input into the global economy. This power shift away from Europe is often used to proclaim the end of the post-war world order and the European socio-economic paradigm. What is often missed out in this account is the second trend: at the same time social democrats are gaining in strength in other regions, most strikingly in Latin America. When we look at both trends, it seems truly self-evident that a complete re-making of the movement is *de facto* a matter of its survival. Socialism had European origins but its future will not be written by Europeans alone.

Both globalisation and post-industrialism have significantly re-shaped the labour market. Globalisation determines the location of labour, imposed above all by worldwide competitiveness of multinational corporations, but we have been here before. The post-industrial era brought new technologies, which – just like the steam engine 200 years ago – entirely redefined the nature of supply chains, industry and services. Social democracy was created as an organising credo for those who worked at the bottom of a production pyramid that was enabled by this industrial revolution. The slogans used back then signify that their core mission was to emancipate the workers and to make sure everyone in society could benefit from progress and personally advance. In the beginning the cause was about the basics, such as worker's safety, limits to working hours, and health insurance, to name a few. Today, all these goals seem to have been achieved in Europe. There is even – in many cases – existing EU legislation, as far as

Social Europe is concerned. So European social democracy faced a double dilemma. It had emancipated a large part of the so called workers class, of which subsequent generations constitute the middle class of today. But trying to reach these emerging classes while not losing support among the contemporary *precariat* – still in need of social protection – social democracy found itself in an impossible bind. On the other hand, the arrangements imposed in the spirit of the welfare state after the Second World War became something all political forces could claim ownership of and subscribe to. In the end, it seemed all in a way became socialists.[7]

Globalisation brought about a necessity for all to face unknown and uncontrollable forces. The recent financial crisis exposed a general inability for rapid, strong and adequate reaction. This encapsulates what has already been widely recognised as a decade of fear – which starting from the dramatic 9/11 attacks, through the war on terror and ending with doomsday news about lethal climate change. It was capitalism that bred individualistic behaviour[8] and it created a multilayer insecurity that induces detachment of people from the communities and societies they live in. This can be seen in the demobilisation and disengagement of people from the world of politics. It is corroding the post-war social contract and makes it impossible to engage in a dialogue about how to restore it and readapt to a changed, multicultural society.

So this is the terrain on which the renewal of social democracy will need to be conducted. It is a process that requires a long-term reflection and thorough reforms of the ways social democracy designs and realises its policies. It must also encompass organisational questions, considering both the internal construction of the progressive movement and the wider perspectives of a broad progressive alliance. All in all, it should be guided by the new mission that social democracy wants to fulfil in the 21st century. The very first principle it should start with is re-defining and restoring the primacy of its core value: equality. This is the conclusion of the interim outcomes of the FEPS Next Left research project.

We must reaffirm that everyone deserves the same opportunities, but also make clear that in exchange everyone must become a part of a global social contract and contribute to its realisation.

The difficulty with this as a founding statement for a new social democratic project is that it seems very abstract, a problem with most debate about ideology and values. This is perhaps a reason why the different political parties' programmes, once they have been put through political marketing mill, often seem all the same to voters.[9] So it is essential to demonstrate the prevailing power of equality as a winning political argument, which can respond to the challenges of globalisation, post-industrialism and individualism.

As outlined above, the recent crisis has exposed the vulnerability of the current world order. The problem is that social democracy has remained within the boundaries of national political stages so far, and so has not been able to propose any true alternative agenda. The historical role of social democracy was to temper capitalism and reconcile it with just labour conditions, but this is a fight that nowadays can only be led at the global level. And it must be guided by the principle of equality. Within the institutional setting, it must be applied in establishing sensible and effective global governance accordingly to the principles of multilateralism. It must be made central to all areas of policy. For example, we should re-engage in the struggle to eradicate poverty worldwide, through measures such as the finalisation of the WTO's trade negotiations round, the implementation of the 'good work' agenda and the elimination of protectionism by wealthy regions. In order to construct such a complex answer to global challenges, we need nothing less than a global social democracy.[10] In order to build one, there is also a particular lesson for

European social democracy to learn, which frequently appeared to hold a superior tone in terms of designing the international agenda. If nothing else, then the different levels of success currently enjoyed by European and Latin American progressives should be a good hint about the need to re-consider.

On a global level, social democrats, even reunited and equipped with a new agenda, cannot fight alone. The last two decades saw the emergence of accelerated activism from the so-called 'alter-globalists', and also civic mobilisations for causes such as the 'make poverty history' campaign or the campaign to free Aung San Suu Kyi. Social democracy has, especially in the first case, been ambiguous in its response to these growing forces of protest. Much of the complaint about its performance was based on the fact that, once it held the power to sit in intergovernmental gatherings, it often sat on the *other side of the barricade* from the trade unions. This must be re-evaluated and seen as a valuable experience that can help to create the worldwide progressive coalitions in the future, in which all have the same rights and duties to both determine the agendas, as also in advocating for them in public.

Applying the equality principle in the post-industrial era will be easiest in the context of a united Europe. It has been pointed out earlier that no state alone is able to exercise a fully fledged sovereignty in defining its own economic and social conditions, neither in good nor in bad times. Paradoxically, social democrats – whose movement was born in the spirit of internationalism – nowadays seem to be the ones most passionately attached to the idea of the individual nation state as the only space in which a welfare state can be operated. But this belief that social policy should remain in the hands of states only is now challenged by the free movement of people, capital, goods and services. We therefore need to work out how to correlate existing welfare models to create an accelerated one on the European level.[11] This is the only way to ensure that all the people in Europe have equal opportunities and that they receive the same, fair treatment as far as social protection, public services and pensions are concerned. This is fundamental to ensure the sustainability of Europe, especially in this current time of crisis in Greece and Ireland, in which bail outs on one side and austerity on the other seem to outrage both pro and anti-Europeans alike. Social democrats naturally must take a leading role in seeking this modern European welfare state that can strengthen EU and protect its people in these difficult times. But for that to happen, it is also essential to go beyond national borders and create a new school of European progressive thought – and this is what Next Left research programme hopes to do.

A strong argument that everyone benefits from equality has been made recently by academics such as Richard Wilkinson and Kate Pickett in *The Spirit Level*, and this provides the right answers to the questions posed by individualism.[12] It is important to uphold the central importance of universalism as we rethink the nature of the European welfare state, which has also been an important theme of recent Fabian research.[13] This is especially vital now that there are those in society who feel that they are no longer bound by 'the social contract' and are therefore not required to contribute, and those that feel they contribute too much. It also needs to be admitted that the welfare state in its original format generated new sorts of inequalities. This situation is made even more complicated by natural changes in society, such as migration or an ageing population. Social democrats must revive the basic principle of equal opportunities for all, but must also find a way to ensure that everyone contributes. This is why the new progressive vision must be accompanied by specific policies. They need to be dedicated to vulnerable groups, such as pensions and health care directed at the elderly or substantial funding for education as the offer to the young. Looking at what has been recently happening on the streets of Paris and London, it is evident that Europe is in desperate need of such an agenda and even more needs to find the ways to legitimise it. To make increased public spending a credible policy, a new economic paradigm is necessary.

The equality agenda is not an easy one to construct, it is a challenging one to promote and it is undeniably tough to execute. Nevertheless this is the unique way that social democracy can reinvent itself, re-establish its position, and regain the legitimacy to act on a political stage. It is not a golden ticket to win elections. On the contrary: it is clear that there are still some elections that social democracy will lose in the near future, especially now that people no longer trust or engage with politicians. But equality and fairness are the principles on which an agenda to restore these relations and to rebuild credibility can be built. Equality is the value that can bring change that will benefit all – it must in the end prevail.

4. After the Crash: A next generation case
Caroline Gennez

A much-repeated analysis of the financial and economic crisis – a crisis of neoliberalism and capitalism – was that it would create an opportunity for centre-left parties. Well, it didn't. Even worse, the majority of social democratic parties have been gasping for breath these last few years. The reason for this is that we didn't connect with the hardship that middle class voters felt during the crisis. To recover, we can write the most beautiful and detailed programme for more European economic and financial cooperation; it won't matter unless we show more emotion and connect better with voters' feelings about our economic policies.

Connecting with the people
At the turn of the century, the centre-left was successful in connecting with what you could call the average voter's feelings. Social democracy was in touch with society. Social democratic parties were regarded as refreshing and modern, partly thanks to the renewal of our parties in Europe that was powered by the Third Way thinking. This was a crucial factor in the electoral success of social democracy all over Europe: 1995 in Portugal, 1997 in the UK and France, 1998 in the Netherlands and Germany, 2003 in Belgium; Tony Blair, Wim Kok, Lionel Jospin, Antonio Guterres, Gerhard Schröder. Those were times when social democratic leaders dominated the European

political stage. Progressives also dominated the political debate. Whether one approves or disapproves of the Third Way, social democratic policy was at the centre of the political debate. One of the key elements was the promise to modernise society and in particular government and public services. We also provided a decisive equalities agenda, with equal rights for gay people, antidiscrimination laws, and legalised euthanasia in some countries. Progressive parties were convincingly in touch with the modern times.

This electoral success had as its foundation solid social and economic policies. Take New Labour: Tony Blair and Gordon Brown restored Labour's economic credibility and invested large sums of money in health care, education and other public services. As Flemish social democrats, we were very successful on social issues during the first liberal and social democratic coalition, the so-called 'purple coalition' in 1999-2003.

But there are more factors involved in losing or winning elections than just the extent to which parties of the left are ready to provide answers to evolving socio-economic conditions, ranging from globalisation to the financial and economic crisis. Despite considerable criticism from the left, not a single social democratic party in Europe has fundamentally deviated from its basic values of solidarity, equal opportunities, redistribution and emancipation. But I don't share the view that there has been a 'betrayal of the left' and we should move more to the left to win elections. In the past, a lot of social democratic parties have moved to the left without resulting in the predicted electoral success.

To put it rather bluntly, social democracy was successful at the end of the nineties and the beginning of the century, not only because we delivered a strong track record on social and economic issues. We were successful because the voter regarded social democrats as a modernising force and, above all, a relevant player. Social democracy captured the moment and could determine the public-political atmosphere. We appealed to the people. We connected with their frame of reference.

We missed the millennium express

If this model helps us to explain our past successes, it could provide an equally applicable explanation for our subsequent defeats. From 2005 onwards, social democracy became more and more out of touch. In the elections that have followed we no longer appealed to voters, especially the centre ground. We no longer delivered the right answers to the challenges of their daily lives.

In government we were confronted with growing budget deficits, ever rising migration numbers, dissatisfaction with multiculturalism, national and international insecurity, fading employment rates, and low pensions combined with high pension costs. The financial and economic crisis made voters even more insecure, while social democratic parties repeated continuously their technocratic solutions or, worse, recalled old-fashioned leftist solutions. Unfortunately, we also made some policy errors which contributed to the perceived 'betrayal of the left'. For example, due to an overly pragmatic approach, in Belgium we introduced a fiscal amnesty. This proposal ran counter to the ethical values of many voters who pay their taxes properly. There are comparable examples for our sister parties across the continent.

Social democracy missed the changing mood in the beginning of this century. Whereas, previously, globalisation had been a theoretical concept for many people, by now everyone could feel its impact. We weren't in touch with the issues people cared about, such as immigration, asylum and integration. Or we avoided talk about these issues and thus didn't tackle them. Or we simply copied right-wing policies to the extent that you can now hardly hear a progressive alternative in Europe.

So, did we deliver a relevant answer to these new challenges? As far as I'm concerned the unequivocal answer is: not sufficiently. No, we were not in the hearts and minds of the people. As far as their values, thoughts and deeds were concerned, we left them indifferent. In other words: we were not with the people and the people were not with us.

Values determined the electoral undercurrent

The absence of strong values was the fundamental flaw of the Third Way or renewed social democratic policies. The Third Way did modernise social democracy in Europe and turned it into a winning formula. But it didn't change the rules of the game. It just copied the right-wing frame of a free market driven society, but improved the policies. You could compare it with the success of Japanese manufacturers in the eighties. But eventually you need creativity and your own framing to maintain success.

We should not underestimate the emotional component of social economic viewpoints or policy. A majority of the population – the average worker or middle class citizen – benefit from redistribution and solidarity, but as a rational argument, this has little impact. If they see themselves as a contributor rather than a beneficiary, we risk losing them altogether as a voter.

A survey of our members gave some interesting results. Three quarters of our members are in favour of the welfare state. When it comes to tackling unemployment though, the same proportion votes for a tougher approach. Taking advantage of the welfare system is seen as a capital sin by our own party. So you could argue in favour of higher social benefits, but at the same time you have to punish people who abuse the system. That's reciprocity. If we don't take this argument into account, middle class voters are immediately up in arms. In Flanders they call it 'hammock socialism'. You could translate that as 'lazy socialism' – it is certainly not a compliment.

We need a sense of urgency

We have to move mountains if social democrats want to return to the centre of the political stage. But it is possible. It's tempting to turn back and cling on to old formulas. But that won't do.

A few ideas spring from the analysis above on how we can change, how we can reignite our mission of building a fair society where life is good, respectful and secure.

First, concerning our social and economic policy, we do need to look beyond the programme's mechanics to the emotional factors and values that are related to welfare, economic growth and social security. People's concerns about their pensions or their children's pensions don't just involve the monthly amount that is transferred to their bank accounts. They are also related to broader questions about the future, such as care, leisure time, housing, safety, and the environment. Another example: when we talk about jobs, we should pay more attention to the experiences that go hand in hand with changing family life and forms of employment. 'A job is the best guarantee against poverty' is a statement that cannot be disputed. Though in the eyes of many hardworking citizens there are numerous other feelings, concerns and questions crying out for an answer: wellbeing in the workplace, how to cope with changing employment terms and conditions or a new management culture, how to combine it all with family life.

In short, which values are hidden behind the need for social progress? And how do we convince the middle class once more of the importance of solidarity? Today the middle class risks paying the bill twice without even realising it. They are seduced by the right-wing stories of fewer taxes, while at the same time the right is advocating no pay rises and no government intervention in the rising cost of living. Nevertheless, whether it is the price of a beer or of health insurance, the middle class pays the bill. It is a real challenge for us to make the middle class realise this imbalance.

Second, our policy range must be increased beyond our core business of social and economic policy. We have to acquire a foothold on new political ground, like migration, integration and security issues. It also requires a more compelling voice and an active practical immersion in areas such as community life and the social environment. In the UK everyone talks about David Cameron's 'Big Society' but the conservatives have stolen a concept and language that ought to belong to the left. For example, Lyndon B. Johnson named his agenda for social improvement the Great Society in the sixties. Let's take this territory back and make it work. We should focus more on people and values, and less on structures.

Subsequently, we should not let ourselves be cornered by the negative feelings or problematic aspects that accompany modern times. We should play a relevant role in the opportunities offered by new times. We have to be involved in shaping the future. If we are bold and creative we can establish links with people and groups that are innovative and entrepreneurial on economic, technical, cultural and ethical levels, as well as on the social level. Social democrats should stand 'with the people' in order to take away their fears and empower their self-confidence. That is what social progress stands for. Entrepreneurs should be considered more as our allies. That is if they are interested in the social context and therefore look beyond pure economic logic.

The question is simple: will social democracy succeed in playing a defining role in modern society? Can we make a positive impact on the processes that shape the future? The answer is as simple as it is daunting: social democracy has to be a force of modernisation – in our own countries, but also at the European level. If we do not succeed in this ambition, we will quite simply cease to be progressive.

5. Economic security and the revival of social Europe
David Coats

Twenty years ago the British centre-left was more enthusiastic about the European project than at any time either before or since. Jacques Delors had addressed the TUC in 1988 and had made the case for a social Europe to complement the single market. His argument was both clear and challenging. In his view, the future prosperity of the continent depended on the opening up and integration of European markets. That was how businesses would survive in a more competitive world, as more countries joined the global trading system and technological change continued to accelerate. Old industries would die and new industries would be born, some occupations would disappear and others rise to new prominence. Expressed in these terms the brave new world looked rather frightening. But Delors was also explicit in saying that unleashing the dynamism of markets had to be matched by a stronger social dimension. Workers had to be participants, not just victims. Information and consultation rights had to be applied across the EU to ensure that workers and their representatives had some influence over the scale and pace of change. A common floor of employment rights was needed to allow the free movement of labour across the EU. And the social partners at both national and European level had a critical role to play in ensuring that the policies responsible for 'creative destruction' were both legitimate and worked to the advantage of all European citizens.

This was an inspiring vision and it encouraged both the Labour Party and the trade unions to embrace the view that the European project, far from being about the creation of a capitalist club, could fulfil progressive goals more effectively than national action alone. Of course, the Delors story has become a little less compelling over time, not least because policymakers have forgotten the elementary lesson that dynamic markets work best with secure and therefore enterprising citizens. There has been far too much concentration on competition, liberalisation and deregulation and far too little focus on employment protection or the quest for consensus. 'Europe' is now more likely to be seen as a source of economic insecurity, not just by Eurosceptics in the UK, but by a wide range of trade unionists and centre-left politicians across the member states. How did this happen? And how can the Delors vision be recovered from the dustbin of history?

The European left in crisis

The problem is especially acute given the weakened condition of the European left today. Social democrats are in power in Greece (just), Spain and Portugal but have experienced recent electoral defeats in the UK, the Netherlands and Sweden. The German SPD appears to be in a state of existential crisis, with their core vote threatened by the Greens and the Left Party. Nicolas Sarkozy may be the most unpopular French president of the last three decades, but there is no sign of great enthusiasm for the Socialist Party. The Italian left, despite Silvio Berlusconi's well known difficulties, looks weak, divided and is struggling to construct a sustainable electoral coalition.

One might find these results puzzling, not least because the global financial crisis seemed to have sounded the death knell for market fundamentalism. But, quite paradoxically, electorates have turned to the centre-right often, as in the UK, to parties that were largely responsible for the emergence of turbo-capitalism and now are implementing austerity policies that could lead to sluggish growth and continued high unemployment, as well as the erosion of the high quality public services on which a dynamic private sector depends.

In 1999, however, at the end of the UK's first presidency of the Council of Ministers under Tony Blair, most of the large countries in the EU had centre-left governments. The third way and triangulation appeared to have been successful electoral strategies in the UK, Germany and the Netherlands. An optimist might have observed that the Delors model of European development shared a great deal with third way thinking. Open and competitive markets combined with strong social policy bore a remarkable resemblance to the New Labour mantra that economic dynamism and social justice were simply two sides of the same coin.

And yet, while the rhetoric sounded similar the practical execution of policy was rather different. So, for example, Gerhard Schroeder's Red-Green coalition in Germany went about the creation of a low wage sector of so-called 'mini jobs' with genuine enthusiasm, believing that this was a necessary condition for full employment. The welfare state was made somewhat less generous and relations with organised labour deteriorated as a result. Income inequality then rose in Germany at a pace similar to that witnessed during the Thatcher-Reagan revolutions in the UK and the USA.

Obviously the position in the UK was slightly different. Tony Blair was deeply committed to the National Minimum Wage and to the introduction of tougher anti-discrimination legislation. But the Government continued to talk about the importance of labour market flexibility using language that was barely a millimetre's distance from the formulas favoured by previous Conservative administrations. And despite the modest tightening of labour market regulation, New Labour initially opposed the information and consultation directive, the agency workers directive and any serious effort to implement the EU limit on working time of 48 hours a week. None of these issues was decisive in influencing voters, but the style and the tone of ministerial pronouncements tended to emphasise flexibility over fairness. One can understand why trade unionists and core voters were more than a little irritated.

A defender of the Government might argue that this was the price that had to be paid for business neutrality. It was better to have a slightly disgruntled CBI accepting most of the Government's (albeit modest) measures than an employer community openly collaborating with the Conservative opposition for the repeal of Labour's employment law reforms. There is some truth in this of course, but there is a wider question about the ultimate failure of *all* the centre-left governments that embraced the fairness and flexibility model, most of whom ended up emphasising the latter at the expense of the former. Contrary to Tony Blair's recent views, clinging to the New Labour orthodoxy is a recipe for continued electoral defeat, not a guaranteed route to victory.

Shaping a new agenda

More than anything else, centre-left parties need to understand why citizens feel anxious and insecure. And we need to accept our share of responsibility too for amplifying some of the causes of insecurity. For far too long it has been accepted that 'globalisation' is a force of nature that is simply unstoppable. On this view, all governments can do is to equip their citizens with the skills they need to find work in an economy characterised by intensifying competition and bewildering change. Yet, and here is another paradox, the essence of social democracy is the belief that market processes can be managed and regulated to benefit all citizens. Our task is not to accept the world as it is and adapt citizens to the demands of the economy, but to reshape the economy to ensure that it serves the interests of citizens.

This means too that we must reject the conflation of the business interest and the public interest. It is simply wrong to believe that whatever is good for corporations (and banks in particular) is good for society. This belief, also embedded in New Labour's DNA and born out of electoral defeat in the 1980s and early 1990s, was demolished by the global financial crisis and the subsequent recession. More than anything else the centre-left in the UK and across Europe needs to return to first principles. Economic credibility depends on the development of a distinctively social democratic political economy that enables us to offer a clear narrative and a convincing prospectus for change. Put more crudely, social democrats across the EU will only win again if they can offer convincing answers to the following four questions: Why is the world the way it is? What's wrong with it? What are we proposing to do about it? And why should the electorate trust us to make the right choices?

Some practical suggestions
A useful starting point is to make a clear statement of the goals of economic policy. Growth must be for a purpose and social democrats desperately need a vision of the good economy. Amartya Sen makes the point well:

"It is simply not adequate to take as our basic objective just the maximization of income or wealth, which is, as Aristotle noted 'merely useful and for the sake of something else'. For the same reason, economic growth cannot sensibly be treated as an end in itself. Development has to be more concerned with enhancing the lives we lead and the freedoms we enjoy. Expanding the freedoms we have reason to value not only makes our lives richer and more unfettered, but also allows us to be fuller social persons, exercising our own volitions and interacting with – and influencing – the world in which we live."

So far as the world of work is concerned, perhaps we need to reinstate what would now be seen as a rather old-fashioned view of the employment relationship, the goals of which might be characterised as *efficiency* (the employer's demand for productivity and performance), *equity* (the worker's demand for fair treatment) and *voice* (respect for the principles of industrial citizenship). Perhaps we can go further and say that it is quite wrong to talk about work-life balance or to make a distinction between work and life at all. A distinctively social democratic political economy will locate the quality of work (and economic security) in a wider politics of the quality of life – which would include concerns about environmental sustainability.

In terms of political strategy this means that Labour must begin to think about work in terms that have been off the agenda for twenty years or more. We must recover the notion of work as craft, as a source of identity, fulfilment and self-respect. We must recognise that change is a constant (not least because technological progress leads to disruptive economic change) but that citizens can be equipped with the capabilities they need to make progress in a more complex world. And we must recognise that the distribution of power in society and in the workplace is of great importance too. In more conventional terms, social democrats must revive the idea that achieving an appropriate balance between capital and labour is one of the fundamental objectives of progressive governance.

Ed Miliband's comprehensive policy review offers a great opportunity to consider how Labour in government can achieve a much higher level of economic security for all citizens. At this stage it is more important to pose questions than offer detailed prescriptions for change. And rather than just rely upon impressions from the doorstep or results from focus groups, it is essential to engage with the electorate in a sustained and sophisticated conversation. We have to listen to what the people have to say.

In the meantime, however, here are some initial questions to shape the developing discussion:

- What needs to be done to create an education and training system that gives young people a sense of occupational identity and self-confidence before they enter the labour market?

- How can learning throughout the life course ensure that workers remain employable and have the capabilities to choose lives that they value?

- What action needs to be taken to ensure that all workers see their wages rise in line with productivity? This is important because those in the 'squeezed middle' have seen no significant improvements in their real earnings since 2005.

- How can workers be given real influence over the decisions that affect them most directly in the workplace?

- If unions are weak in the private sector then what should government do (if anything) to encourage the growth of countervailing power to the unconstrained exercise of employer prerogatives?

- What further changes to the welfare system are needed to return to a high employment rate with decent work available for all those capable of work?

- Where should government intervene and how should employer behaviour be regulated and, in particular, can the reform of company law (directors' duties, reporting requirements) create a different set of incentives for employers to offer high quality, sustainable, fulfilling work?

These are questions of relevance to social democrats across Europe. While national situations are all slightly different, there is a generalised anxiety about the future, about the security of employment, about the fairness (and generosity) of welfare states and about whether the next generation can expect higher living standards and more opportunity. The task of social democracy is to offer an optimistic prospect that is rooted in the harsh realities of the world as it is. Answering these demands with clarity and conviction is the best route to the resurgence of the centre-left and the revival of the Delors ambition for a genuinely social Europe.

6. Learning from the Eurosceptics
Jessica Asato

A pro-European looking at successful European campaigns run in Britain over the last decade would be forgiven for being despondent. After all, one of the single most dramatic campaign failures was the 'Britain in Europe' campaign which was launched with large amounts of money and cross-party support, only to die a sad death a few years later. The European Movement does not live up to its name. There is no movement to speak of. In truth it is hard to point to a pro-European campaign in the UK making any impact at all.

The easy answer is to blame the miserable reception for Europhile messages on Britain's Eurosceptic media which makes any debate about Europe so difficult. But rarely do pro-European campaigns ask themselves why they aren't doing better or what can they learn from anti-European campaigns or other successful progressive campaigns.

Anti-European campaigns are characterised by being located as close as possible to the man in the Dog and Duck. They pick symbolic everyday issues which have resonance with people who are already fearful of change. Hence the successful use of straight bananas and other Euro-myths which have become embedded in the popular imagination. Pro-European campaigns on the other hand have always struggled to translate support for an abstract concept – Europe – into bread and butter politics. Partly this has been because most energy recently has gone into campaigning for a Euro referendum and for the Lisbon

Treaty, which meant that the wider case for 'Europe' as a good in people's lives has been mostly ignored.

The new polling conducted by YouGov for this collection bears this out and shows the power of making specific arguments rather than abstract ones. Despite 45 per cent of people thinking Britain's membership of the EU is a "bad thing", 55 per cent want closer co-operation on climate change, 53 per cent on regulating banks, and 45 per cent on economic recovery. Pro-Europeans *can* argue with the grain of public opinion.

It could also be argued, however, that pro-Europeans have deliberately framed their campaigns to invoke a feeling about being part of a European community or identity, rather than hanging them on single issues which affect daily lives. Arguments are commonly made about the need for Europe to stop a third world war, or to tackle climate change, or to facilitate cross-border co-operation. All well and good, but a hostile public can quickly discount the importance of any of these issues to their lives either because they are unlikely (world war), too big (climate change) or too far away (borders).

Anti-Europeans are better at picking arguments with Europe which will affect the way people live, or how they perceive they live. So the idea of 'Brussels bureaucrats' taking away British people's right to drink out of a pint glass takes hold even though it has little basis in reality, simply because it threatens people's way of life. Pro-Europeans need to get better at identifying European issues which people can relate to. Animal welfare is a good one, but so too are longer holidays and mobile phone charges. Pro-Europeans need to exploit the occasions in the future where the Government tries to water down rights which have been negotiated with the European Union. They also need to be far more vocal at campaigning for the Government to support progressive European legislation. Not only does this help to make the case for Europe, but also binds people into legislative change at a

European level rather than simply at a state level.

Second, anti-Europeans are better at mobilising people. The Democracy Movement's 'Stop the Eurostate' rally in London in 2000 was a good example; today, their website has a campaign hotline and features pictures of activists on street stalls prominently on its front page. It has an interactive map which allows readers to get in touch with their local campaign organiser. In contrast, the European Movement's website is more about giving people information about Europe, rather than actively campaigning for Britain to remain in Europe. Nowhere, except in the Young European Movement's pages, does it ask the reader to do something proactive.

Yet the internet gives pro-Europeans a great arena to mobilise people. As we move towards greater citizen-led democracy online, it would be a good idea for pro-Europeans to organise from the grassroots online. At the moment engagement is very much led from the top, with politicians expected to give the steer and the people to follow. Online campaigning organisations such as Avaaz.org and its sister in Britain, 38 Degrees, show that progressive issues can be forced on politicians and the media if ordinary people feel engaged.

In fact the fundamental mistake which made the 'Britain in Europe' campaign doomed from the start was to let Government and senior politicians give the lead on the Euro. Not only did it mean the whole campaign rested on the ability of the Labour Government to win over a mainly Eurosceptic press – which was very unlikely to happen – it also allowed the No Campaign to immediately stereotype them as being politicians for the politicians. The No Campaign instead launched with celebrities, comedians and 'popular' politicians such as Denis Healey and David Owen, rather than people who could be pigeon-holed as part of the institution.

Pro-Europeans have always made the mistake of thinking that they are the 'insiders', when in fact the dominance of the Eurosceptic media makes them the outsiders. Instead of high-level policy meetings and campaigns with politicians, the tactics should be noisy, irreverent and led by citizen activists. The ability to grow mass email lists which speak directly to people; to use social media such as Twitter and Facebook to regularly expose right-wing myths about Europe; or to be able to create viral videos which show how the very rich control the debate about Europe to project their own interests, should all be of benefit to pro-European campaigns which find it hard to gain a foothold in the mainstream media. Eddie Izzard, who is a well-known supporter of Europe, has 1.7 million Twitter followers – when he supports a campaign it has the potential to reach far more ordinary people than traditional campaigns among people who have signed on the dotted line.

This doesn't mean, however, that pro-European campaigners should avoid involvement with the media altogether. If anything, there are too few pro-European voices in the media and more effort should be made to ensure that it is easy for journalists to find them. If one looks at organisations such as the Taxpayer's Alliance, for example, they are so media focused that a contact mobile number for journalists is featured right on the home page. Pro-Europeans need to get away from the idea that because journalists are part of the problem they should be ignored until they grow up. Pro-European blogs with good links to senior journalists could help to drive stories in papers which still remain broadly supportive of Europe such as *The Guardian*, *The Mirror* and *The Independent*.

Pro-Europeans also need to reach out to other campaigns which might share the same objectives. The green movement is an obvious partner, as are the trade unions, with their emphasis on workers' rights. Active steps are needed to work jointly on campaigns to extend their reach and recognise that the most effective campaigns have many stakeholders who touch thousands of supporters. The campaign to oppose a referendum on electoral reform in 2011 is instructive as it combines both the Taxpayer's Alliance and people involved with Business for Sterling and the No Campaign. Neither of these issues at first instance would seem to have much to do with electoral reform, but both can garner huge lists of supporters and media clout. Building a big base of supporters will be key to keeping pro-European organisations going since they lack the financial backing which many Eurosceptic organisations have. Online fundraising is only in its infancy in the UK, but as Hope Not Hate showed, there is potential for single issue campaigns to raise significant money with small donations.

Finally, there is still a need to campaign within political parties to get support for Europe. At the end of the day, politicians will run scared of the issue unless they feel they have enough support both with the public, but also in their party. The Labour Party has failed to have a genuine debate about its approach to Europe ever since the campaign to join the euro failed. Healthy internal pro-European organisations are more important than ever to convince the next generation of political activists that the European dream is one worth fighting for.

The last decade may have seen the decline of pro-European campaigns, but the new opportunities offered by online campaigning and a change of Government could see a more successful decade ahead. But pro-Europeans need to reach out to the public, find issues which resonate and make pacts with other organisations to extend their reach if they are to succeed.

7. Polling: what the British really think about Europe

It is important to know the lie of the land; the post-crisis case for Europe must be based on the realities of post-crisis attitudes. The YouGov polling conducted for this pamphlet is a mixed bag but not a curate's egg: there is good and bad news, but the European cause is far from a write-off.

As would be expected, a decade of debates centred on institutional wrangling combined with recent financial and political turmoil, have hardened general attitudes against the European Union, and the idea of any closer co-operation between the 27 states receives short shrift. This shows how highfalutin attempts to appeal to the ideal of a common European citizenry have fallen on deaf ears. The best advice when in a hole is to stop digging.

But across all categories – class, gender, age, political affiliation – there is significant support for combined European action when it is to tackle the key political challenges of the day, highlighting a bedrock of popular support for pro-Europeans to build on – if the EU can prove itself to be practically useful in specific areas and relevant to people's lives.

It might be that campaigning not in poetry but in prose is the best way of showing the public there are practical benefits to Europe.

Good or bad?

> Is Britain's membership of the European
> Union a good thing or a bad thing for
> Britain?
>
> | | % |
> |---|---|
> | *Good thing* | **22** |
> | *Bad thing* | **45** |
> | *Neither good nor bad* | **21** |
> | *Don't know* | **12** |

There is a stark class gap in attitudes to the EU. 53 per cent of C2DE voters say it is a bad thing overall, and only 13 per cent a good thing overall – a gap of 40 points. However, among ABC1 voters the gap closes to 12 points, with 28 per cent positive and 40 per cent negative. Narrow pluralities of Labour supporters (35 per cent to 34 per cent) and LibDem supporters (36 per cent to 27 per cent) are positive about the EU, while Conservatives are strongly negative (15 per cent to 61 per cent).

Only 16 per cent of women say the EU is a good thing, compared to 28 per cent of men. Men are also more likely to say it is a bad thing (48 per cent) than women (43 per cent). 23 per cent of women say it is neither a good nor bad thing, while three times as many women (18 per cent) as men say they don't know.

The 27 countries

The 27 countries in the European Union work together in different ways.
Thinking about Europe as a whole, rather just Britain, what is your view of the level of cooperation between EU countries?

%

Overall, the EU member states should **21**
co-operate more closely so that they can better
deal with major international issues

Overall, the EU member states should loosen **49**
their links so they have more flexibility to deal
with national issues

Overall, the current balance between EU **9**
co-operation and national action is about right

Don't know **20**

Supporters of all the major political parties prefer looser EU co-operation overall. While 66 per cent of Conservatives favour looser ties, with 15 per cent favouring closer co-operation, the margins in favour of looser ties are narrower among Labour (40 per cent to 30 per cent) and LibDem (38 per cent to 33 per cent) voters.

Closer co-operation?

Below is a list of specific areas. For each one please say whether you think countries in Europe should co-operate more closely together, or should loosen their links or if the present balance is about right.

Tackling climate change   %

EU countries should co-operate   **55**
more closely on this issue

EU countries should loosen their links   **14**
on this issue

The current balance is about right   **14**

Don't know   **16**

Diplomatic relations with non-European countries (such as sharing embassies)

EU countries should co-operate   **35**
more closely on this issue

EU countries should loosen their links   **26**
on this issue

The current balance is about right   **17**

Don't know   **22**

Cont...

Fighting terrorism & international crime

EU countries should co-operate more closely on this issue   **71**

EU countries should loosen their links on this issue   **7**

The current balance is about right   **9**

Don't know   **13**

Regulating banks and financial institutions

EU countries should co-operate more closely on this issue   **53**

EU countries should loosen their links on this issue   **25**

The current balance is about right   **6**

Don't know   **15**

Recovering from the recession and financial crisis

EU countries should co-operate more closely on this issue   **45**

EU countries should loosen their links on this issue   **30**

The current balance is about right   **9**

Don't know   **16**

Closer co-operation on climate change has support across all parties, with Conservatives in favour by 50 per cent to 22 per cent, alongside 66 per cent 67 per cent of Labour and LibDem voters. Those who say the EU is a bad thing overall want closer co-operation on climate change by 48 per cent to 24 per cent.

Closer co-operation in regulating banks has the backing of Conservatives (45 per cent to 38 per cent) and those who think British membership of the EU is a bad thing (48 per cent to 37 per cent), along with very strong support (74 per cent to 11 per cent) among those who are positive about the EU. There is 54 per cent support from C2DE supporters, along with 53 per cent of ABC1 voters.

On recovery from the recession, Conservative voters, who oppose closer cooperation by 37 per cent to 44 per cent disagree with both Labour (59 per cent to 21 per cent) and Liberal Democrat (48 per cent to 26 per cent) supporters on this.

Minimum levels of workers rights

Do you think the European Union should agree minimum levels of levels of workers rights so EU countries cannot undercut each other with cheaper labour or lower regulation, or should each country be able to make their own decisions about what regulations are best for their workers.

	%
The European Union should agree minimum levels of workers' rights	**55**
The European Union should not agree minimum levels of workers' rights	**27**
Don't know	**17**

This has equally strong support from ABC1 (56 per cent) and C2DE (54 per cent) voters, and is favoured by Conservatives (48 per cent to 42 per cent) as well as Labour (71 per cent to 16 per cent) and LibDem (66 per cent to 20 per cent) voters. It is also supported by those who think EU membership a bad thing (49 per cent to 41 per cent) or who are neutral about it (54 per cent to 25 per cent) as well as among pro-EU voters (76 per cent to 15 per cent), suggesting it is an issue which could help to address concerns about the EU.

Minimum levels of taxation

Do you think the European Union should agree minimum levels of taxation on large businesses so companies cannot relocate to whichever countries offer the lowest tax rates, or should each country be able to make their own decisions about what level of tax is best for their companies.

	%
The European Union should agree minimum levels of tax on large businesses	**47**
The European Union should not agree minimum levels of tax on large businesses	**34**
Don't know	**19**

Labour (59 per cent to 26 per cent) and Liberal Democrat (56 per cent to 30 per cent) voters agree with this proposal but most Conservatives oppose it (36 per cent to 52 per cent). There is stronger support among C2DE voters (48 per cent to 30 per cent) than ABC1 voters (46 per cent to 38 per cent).

Financial transactions tax

Q Some people have suggested a Europe-wide tax of 0.05% on financial trades (such as buying and selling shares, derivatives and foreign currencies), claiming it would stabilise economies and raise funds from financial speculation. Other people think this would be unworkable, or fear it would lead to big banks and financial institutions re-locating to other countries without a transaction tax.

Which of the following best reflects your view?

	%
The European Union should introduce a tax on financial transactions, even if other countries do not agree	**15**
The European Union should only introduce a tax on financial transactions if there is a global agreement to introduce it	**27**
The European Union should not introduce a tax on financial transactions	**29**
Don't know	**30**

Those who think that British membership of the EU is a good thing are much happier with the idea of introducing a tax unilaterally – among this group support rises to 28 per cent. 44 per cent of Conservative voters think the EU shouldn't introduce a tax, compared to 19 per cent of Labour voters.

The rise of China

Thinking about the next 25 years or so, many people have suggested that China will join the United States as a second political and economic Superpower. If that turns out to be true, which of the following is closest to your view.

%

Britain and other European countries should **40** *work more closely together to maximise their voice and influence in the world.*

Britain and other European countries should **33** *use their own historic international links to try to maximise their own voice and influence.*

Neither **9**

Don't know **18**

Both Labour (54 per cent to 25 per cent) and LibDem voters (55 per cent to 23 per cent) believe the rise of China should see closer EU cooperation, but Conservatives are more likely to disagree (30 per cent to 47 per cent).

Endnotes

Chapter 3 (Alfred Gusenbauer)

1   Sheri Berman, *The Primacy of Politics*, Cambridge University Press 2006, p.12 and following pages.

2   Jenny Andersson, *Social Democracy and Capitalism in the Knowledge Age*, Stanford University Press 2010, p. 148.

3   Sigmar Gabriel, Chair of SPD suggests that the political centre is defined each time and calls upon social democracy to seek this *prerogative of interpretation*. See: Sigmar Gabriel, Chairman of Sozialdemokratische Partei Deutschlands (SPD). Speech delivered at the SPD Federal Party Convention in Dresden on 13th November 2009, [in:] E. Stetter, K. Duffek, A. Skrzypek, *Next Left – The Leaders' Visions for Europe's Future*, FEPS Brussels 2010, p. 26-53.

4   Ashley Lavelle, *The Death of Social Democracy – Political Consequences in 21st Century*, Ashgate 2008 p.169 and following pages.

5   Donald Sassoon, 'Socialism in the twentieth century', [in:] Ed. J. Callaghan and I. Favretto, *Transitions in Social Democracy: Cultural and ideological problems of the Golden Age*, Manchester University Press 2006, p. 15-34.

6   Thomas Meyer, Luis Hinchman, *The Theory of Social Democracy*, Polity Cambridge 2008, p.175-180.

7   Tony Judt, *Ill Fares the Land*, Penguin London 2010, p.6.

8   Robert D. Putnam, *Bowling Alone: The collapse and revival of American Community*, Simon and Schuster New York 2000

9   Nina Fishman, Afterword, in ed. J. Callaghan, N. Fishman, B. Jackson, M. McIvor, *In Search of Social Democracy: Responses to crisis and modernisation*, Manchester University Press 2009, p. 286-287.

10 Peter Evans, *From Situations of Dependency to Globalized Social Democracy*, published at www.springerlink.com; materials of the Next Left Colloquium organised on 29th-20th September 2010 by Watson Institute of Brown University, Providence (RI), USA.

11 See also: *Welfare States in Transition*. National adaptations in global economies. Ed. G. Esping-Andersen, UNISB London 2004.

12 See: R. Wilkinson, K. Pickett, *The Spirit Level. Why equality is better for everyone*, Penguin London 2010.

13 Tim Horton and James Gregory *The Solidarity Society: Why we can afford to end poverty, and how to do it with public support*, Fabian Society 2009.

Endnotes

Discussion Guide: Europe's Left in the Crisis

How to use this Discussion Guide

The guide can be used in various ways by Fabian Local Societies, local political party meetings and trade union branches, student societies, NGOs and other groups.

■ You might hold a discussion among local members or invite a guest speaker – for example, an MP, academic or local practitioner to lead a group discussion.

■ Some different key themes are suggested. You might choose to spend 15 – 20 minutes on each area, or decide to focus the whole discussion on one of the issues for a more detailed discussion.

A discussion could address some or all of the following questions:

1. The crisis of Europe's left: a common challenge

How far do the political and electoral challenges faced by the major European centre-left parties have common causes, rather than being nationally distinctive?

How can comparative analysis across the EU help national parties with their political challenges? Where is a shared European agenda desirable?

2. A new political economy

Why has the centre-left struggled to win arguments about the economic response to the crisis – and what explains the success of the European centre-right in framing arguments about austerity?

How can a social democratic agenda on addressing economic insecurity be translated into both policies and public arguments?

3. Winning public arguments for internationalism

If social democracy in one country is impossible, how can the centre-left win public consent and support for closer international cooperation at a time when political disengagement is high, both nationally and particularly with regard to the EU and other multilateral fora?

Polling conducted for this pamphlet shows public scepticism towards European integration in the abstract, but also the opportunity to win support for closer cooperation in a range of specific areas. Can this insight help to support successful advocacy and campaigning – and what messages and approach should inform it?

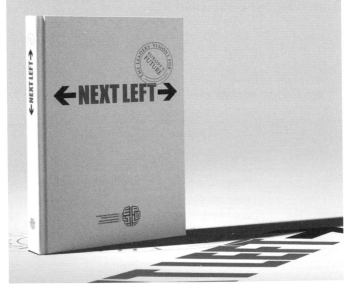

JOIN BRITAIN'S ONLY MEMBERSHIP THINK TANK

Members of the Fabian Society receive at least four pamphlets or books a year as well as our quarterly magazine, 'Fabian Review'. You'll also receive invitations to special members' events and regular lectures and debates with leading politicians and thinkers.

For just £9.95 you can join now for six months and we'll send you two pamphlets and the latest magazine free.

Call 020 7227 4900, email us at info@fabian-society.org.uk, or go to www.fabians.org.uk for more information.

Is Equality Fair?

What the public really think about equality – and what we should do about it.

Edited by Tom Hampson and Jemima Olchawski

In this Fabian Special, John Denham, Kate Green, Stewart Lansley, Jemima Olchawski, Ben Page and Zoe Williams respond to new Fabian work on public attitudes to fairness.

The work, commissioned by the Joseph Rowntree Foundation, found that most people think that 'deserved' inequalities are fair, and attitudes towards those on low incomes were often more negative than attitudes towards the rich. However, we also found that people strongly support progressive tax and benefits.

"If we ever give up on fairness and equality the centre left will have lost all meaning. The Fabian research on voter attitudes doesn't tell us to give up; it just asks us to think about how we move forward." – John Denham MP

The Solidarity Society

Why we can afford to end poverty, and how to do it with public support.

Tim Horton and James Gregory

This report sets out a strategy for how to reduce, eliminate and prevent poverty in Britain.

'The Solidarity Society' is the final report of a project to commemorate the centenary of Beatrice Webb's 1909 Minority Report of the Royal Commission on the Poor Law. It addresses how the values and insights of the Minority Report can animate and inspire a radical contemporary vision to fight and prevent poverty in modern Britain.

The report makes immediate proposals to help build momentum for deeper change. It also seeks to learn lessons from the successes and failures of post-war welfare history, as well as from international evidence on poverty prevention.

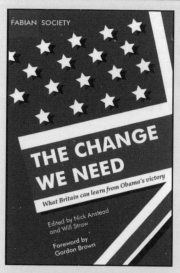

The Change We Need

What Britain can learn from Obama's victory

Edited by Nick Anstead and Will Straw, with a foreword by Gordon Brown

How can a party in office for more than a decade recapture its idealism? Can Labour hope to draw on the same popular enthusiasm that swept Barack Obama to victory?

In 'The Change We Need', staffers from the Obama campaign come together with senior British and American politicians, academics, thinkers and campaigners to draw forwardlooking and optimistic lessons for the British progressive left. Together they show that the opportunity can only be seized if we fundamentally rethink the ways we do politics in Britain, by rejecting the command-and-control model of the New Labour era and energising grassroots supporters.

"Contained within these pages are the ideas of tomorrow – the new ways of working that will help Labour members do even more to change our world." – Gordon Brown

JOIN THE FABIANS TODAY

Join us and receive at least four pamphlets or books a year as well as our quarterly magazine, 'Fabian Review'.

I'd like to become a Fabian for just £9.95

I understand that should at any time during my six-month introductory membership period I wish to cancel, I will receive a refund and keep all publications received without obligation. After six months I understand my membership will revert to the annual rate as published in *Fabian Review*, currently £33 (ordinary) or £16 (unwaged).

Name	Date of birth
Address	
	Postcode
Email	
Telephone	

Instruction to Bank   Originator's ID: 971666

Bank/building society name	**DIRECT Debit**
Address	
	Postcode
Acct holder(s)	
Acct no.	Sort code

I instruct you to pay direct debits from my account at the request of the Fabian Society. The instruction is subject to the safeguards of the Direct Debit Guarantee.

Signature	Date

Return to:
Fabian Society Membership
FREEPOST SW 1570
11 Dartmouth Street, London SW1H 9BN